ROWAN

presents

crochet
workshop

ROWAN

presents

crochet
workshop

The Complete Course for the Beginner to Intermediate Crocheter

Emma Seddon & Sharon Brant

Technical editor Sally Harding
Photography John Heseltine

TRAFALGAR SQUARE
North Pomfret, Vermont

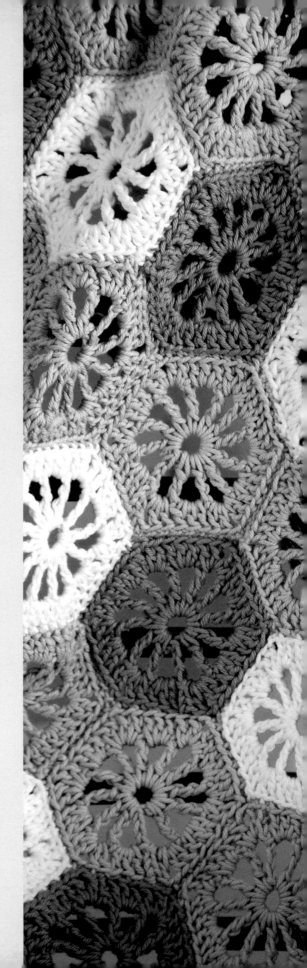

 R O W A N

presents

crochet
workshop

First published in the United States of American in 2008 by
Trafalgar Square Books, North Pomfret, Vermont 05053

Reproduced in Singapore and printed in China

Copyright © Rowan Yarns 2008

Rowan consultant Sharon Brant
Technical editor Sally Harding
Designer Anne Wilson
Pattern checkers Penny Hill and Sue Whiting
Crocheters Emma Seddon and Carole Downie
Stylist Susan Berry
Index Marie Lorimer

Library of Congress Control Number: 2008900776

ISBN: 978-1-57076-397-7

10 9 8 7 6 5 4 3 2 1

contents

Introduction

Although crochet has often been regarded as a pastime fit only for grannies, a batch of new young designers have succeeded in making it "cool," with some beautiful designs in stunning yarns. Crochet lends itself particularly well to accessories and homeware, making great bags, wonderful throws, and funky pillows. It can also be used for some fantastic garments, but, as a fabric, it drapes slightly less well than knitting, so it is important to understand the vast potential as well as the minor limitations of crochet as a fabric.

Learning to crochet

Compared with knitting, however, crochet is quick to work—it grows fast. It is also a convenient craft as it requires only one small hook, so you can carry it around and work it on trains, boats, and planes, or whenever and wherever you have time to spare. Like knitting, crochet is a form of yoga. The repetitive nature of the stitching is soothing, and the fact that you are creating something beautiful is therapeutic, too.

Learning to crochet, like learning to knit, is easiest when taught one to one, and because of this Rowan have run workshop groups for both knitters and

BELOW Women attending an Intermediate Crochet workshop at the Mill at Rowan Yarns in West Yorkshire.

crocheters for many years. This book is intended as a comprehensive backup, offering all the skills and techniques to take you up to intermediate level. At this level you will be able to read a pattern, work different stitches, shape your crochet, and stitch the pieces together successfully.

You will find, as with any new skill, that it takes a little time to become confident. It is important when learning to crochet to take it step by step in order to develop an even, relaxed style. This will allow you to produce regular stitches that are neither too loose nor too tight to work in and out of with ease.

Very soon, you will be able to make simple and attractive small projects, and each success will lead you to try something a little more adventurous next time.

As you gain confidence, you will start to see that although our workshops take you down a particular path, there are plenty of highways and byways, where you can develop your own creative skills: choosing your own colors and maybe trying out different stitches.

Using this book

Although the book is divided into six workshops, you will find in practice that you can "pick and mix" according to your needs.

Workshop One gets you started on the basic—and most commonly used—crochet stitches, and by the end of this section you should be able to work a piece of plain crochet in half a dozen stitches. The little coaster project is a good test of your basic skills.

Workshop Two introduces you to the idea of adding color to straight pieces of crochet, so you can add stripes of color, or join in new yarns. It shows you how to join pieces of crochet together and also how to edge both crochet and other fabrics with simple decorative edgings. A simple stripy scarf and a patched pillow cover offer you the chance to practice your skills.

Workshop Three gets you going on shaping crochet, so you can make simple triangles. It also shows you how to work round and round and how to work different stitches and colors in the round—so that you can make the wonderful pieced throws, known as afghans, in different colors and yarns.

Workshop Four teaches you a range of different crochet stitch types: simple textured stitches, fancy decorative stitches, and lacy ones. It also takes your color skills on to another level so you can work fancy jacquard patterns, where different colors are used in one row.

Workshop Five introduces you to garment making, firstly with a simple, quick-to-make baby jacket and dress, and then to an adult cardigan. This section also explains garment "fit"—how to make sure your crocheted sweater fits just right.

Workshop Six takes you into associated areas of crochet including stitch embellishment, using beads, and felting your crochet.

Troubleshooting tips

Tip boxes like this appear throughout the book. Pay particular attention to these tips because they give good advice to beginners and experienced crocheters alike.

Yarn and equipment

You will need some basic equipment to get started on crochet but fortunately, you don't need much. To get practicing, just pick up a couple of balls of lightweight yarn and a medium-size hook (see Troubleshooting Tips on page 18).

Yarns for crochet

Well, you can crochet with pretty much anything that is flexible, from wire to yak hair. Most people, however, prefer to crochet with the yarns made by manufacturers for the purpose. These yarns are created by spinning the strands (known as plies) of fibers together.

It is important when choosing a yarn type, to make sure it is fit for the purpose. Also, as you are going to be handling it a lot, you need to enjoy the way the yarn feels, and like the way it works up into a crochet fabric. Will it form a flexible, springy fabric or one that is flat and characterless? Another important issue is: will it wash and wear well?

Manufactured yarns are natural, synthetic, or a mixture of the two. The natural yarns include silk,

cotton, wool, bamboo, hemp, and linen. Wool varies greatly according the animal, or breed of animal, from which it is obtained. Cashmere (from goats) is very soft. Merino wool is also soft—not as soft as cashmere, but much springier. To get the best of all possible worlds, and the benefits of the attributes of different yarn types, manufacturers often combine them in different proportions. Not all natural yarns are machine washable, and some, particularly cashmere and softer yarns, shrink readily in very hot water. This, however, is a useful characteristic when it comes to felting!

Synthetic yarns are produced from man-made fibers. These include acrylic, rayon, polyester, and nylon. Generally less expensive than natural fibers, they are also useful for their durability, and washability. However, they often lack the luster and elasticity of natural fibers, and frequent washing can render them lackluster.

Novelty yarns are composed of a range of materials, and include metallics and fake fur yarns.

BELOW The Rowan yarns on display in the Rowan Mill include wools, cottons, silks, alpaca, and various mixes.

Buying yarn

Most yarns come with a printed yarn label. Rowan yarns, for example, offer the standard information on each ball of yarn. Their yarn labels are geared for knitters rather than the crocheters, but most of the information is useful to crocheters, too (see pages 186–188). It includes:

- Weight of the ball
- Yardage/meterage in the ball
- Recommended knitting needle size to use with the yarn
- Number of stitches and rows per 4in (10cm) square worked in stockinette stitch
- Recommended washing method
- Color shade number
- Color dye lot number

When buying yarn for a particular project, make sure that each ball not only carries the same shade number, but also carries the same dye lot number, as batches of dye can vary enough to be visible in the finished project.

BELOW These sheep are in a field behind the Rowan Mill in Holmfirth, West Yorkshire. The valleys in this area have long been renowned for yarn spinning and dyeing.

Equipment

The basic equipment you need for crochet is minimal, and if you crochet (or sew), you will probably have many of the tools required in your workbasket already.

Crochet hooks

There is a wide range of sizes and types of crochet hook. Take your time to try a few types of hook—plastic, metal, or wood—to see which one is the most comfortable for you.

The very finest hook sizes are used for working intricate lace stitches and the really fat ones for bulky yarns (which, of course, make for fast work). Most contemporary patterns call for the medium range of sizes—from a size B-1 (2mm) to a size N-13 (9mm).

Other equipment

Aside from hooks, here are the other simple tools and equipment you will need.

Scissors: A sharp pair of scissors with a good point are essential for cutting yarn and sewing seams.

Ruler and tape measure: These are for measuring your gauge swatches and your finished crochet.

Pins: Rustproof stainless steel pins come in handy for pinning out crochet when blocking pieces and for pinning seams together.

Stitch markers: Your instructions will sometimes ask you to mark a position on the crochet. For this, you can use manufactured ring markers, safety pins, or simply a short length of contrasting thread or yarn.

Blunt-ended yarn needles: Large-eyed blunt-ended needles are essential for sewing together crocheted pieces. A blunt-ended needle will not split the yarn.

Notebook: Keep a ring-bound notebook for yarn swatches and to make notes when working on your crochet. A pinboard above a desk is useful for studying swatches and color samples.

Tote bag: Until you can crochet your own, make sure you have a tote bag for your crochet and equipment, to keep it all safely in one place and, equally important, to keep your work clean!

Hook conversion chart

This chart shows how the various hook-size systems compare. The closest equivalents are lined up across the column; they are not always exactly the same size, but are close enough in size to be substituted for each other.

European metric	US	old UK
.60mm	14 steel	
.75mm	12 steel	
1mm	11 steel	
1.25mm	7 steel	
1.50mm	6 steel	
1.75mm	5 steel	
2mm	B-1	14
2.5mm	C-2	12
3mm	D-3	10
3.5mm	E-4	9
	F-5	
4mm	G-6	8
4.5mm	7	7
5mm	H-8	6
5.5mm	I-9	5
6mm	J-10	4
6.5mm	K-10 1/2	3
7mm		2
8mm	L-11	
9mm	N-13	
10mm	P-15	
12mm		
16mm	Q	
20mm	S	

Language of crochet

The language of crochet is probably the most off-putting part for beginners. They take one look at a crochet pattern with all its abbreviations, gasp and think, I can never understand all that!

In this book, we have chosen to introduce you to crochet terms and abbreviations little by little, only introducing those that are necessary to the point at which you are working. However, it is important to understand that a crochet pattern is just a detailed written or visual instruction manual for the project you are about to embark on.

Types of instructions

As with all forms of communication, there are different ways of expressing crochet: in writing (i.e., with abbreviations) or with special visual symbols. Here are three versions of a very simple crochet pattern for a simple rectangle in single crochet.

The pattern written out in full

Written out in full, the instructions would read:
Make a foundation chain of 11 chain stitches.
Row 1 Work one single crochet stitch into the second chain from the hook, then work one single crochet into each of the remaining chains. Turn the work so

---

The "foundation row"

Some crochet patterns call the first row of crochet—the row worked onto the foundation chain—the "foundation row." To avoid confusion and make the instructions simpler to understand, this book follows the standard style of calling this row "row 1."

---

you are ready to begin the next row. You now have 10 single crochet stitches in the row.
Row 2 Work one chain stitch for the "turning chain," then work one single crochet into the top of each stitch in the previous row. Turn the work.
Rows 3 and 4 Repeat row 2 twice more.
Cut the yarn and pull the end through the loop on the hook. Pull the yarn end to tighten the loop.

The pattern written in crochet-speak

This is abbreviated into crochet-speak as follows:
Ch 11.
Row 1 1 sc in 2nd ch from hook, 1 sc in each of rem ch, turn. *10 sc.*
Row 2 1 ch, 1 sc in each sc to end of row, turn.
Rows 3 and 4 Rep row 2 twice. Fasten off.

The pattern written in crochet symbols

The same pattern is written in symbols (see opposite page) as follows:

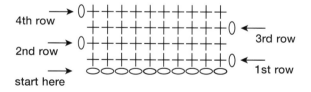

So you see, you can explain crochet written out in full, or in shorthand with abbreviations or symbols.

Each shorthand method has its proponents, but often the two are combined. For example, a the repeat of a textured stitch pattern may be given in symbols along side the row-by-row written instructions for beginning, shaping, and finishing a garment.

Charts are also sometimes used for crochet. For example for filet crochet (see page 117), jacquard crochet (see pages 126–127), or beaded crochet (see page 171).

Following crochet patterns

Here are the main crochet abbreviations and symbols, plus special information about US and UK terms. See page 137 for more about following garment patterns.

Crochet terminology

This book uses the US crochet terminology. It differs from UK terminology as follows:

US	UK
single crochet (sc)	= double crochet (dc)
half double crochet (hdc)	= half treble crochet (htr)
double crochet (dc)	= treble crochet (tr)
triple (tr)	= double treble (dtr)
double treble (dtr)	= triple treble (trtr)
triple treble (trtr)	= quadruple treble (qtr)
yarn over (yo)	= yarn round hook (yrh)
skip	= miss
slip stitch (sl st)	= slip stitch (ss)

Crochet symbols

Crochet symbol instructions are very easy to follow as they have been developed to echo the relative sizes, shapes, and positions of the actual stitches. Most crochet patterns can be written out in symbols. There are even special symbols for complicated stitches and for working increases and decreases.

The symbols used to represent individual crochet stitches vary from country to country, but the crochet book you are using will always provide a key to all the symbols that appear in the patterns. In English-language books the most commonly used crochet symbols for the basic crochet stitches are:

◯ = chain stitch

• = slip stitch

+ = single crochet

T = half double crochet

⊤ = double crochet

⨎ = treble crochet

Crochet abbreviations

These are the main abbreviations used in crochet patterns.

alt	alternate
beg	begin(ning)
ch	chain
cm	centimeter(s)
cont	continu(e)(ing)
dc	double crochet
dec	decreas(e)(ing)
DK	double knitting (a lightweight yarn)
dtr	double treble
foll	follow(s)(ing)
g	gram(s)
hdc	half double crochet
in	inch(es)
inc	increase(e)(ing)
lp(s)	loop(s)
m	meter(s)
mm	millimeter(s)
oz	ounce(s)
patt	pattern; or work in pattern
rem	remain(s)(ing)
rep	repeat(s)(ing)
RS	right side
sc	single crochet
sp(s)	space(s)
ss	slip stitch
st(s)	stitch(es)
t-ch	turning chain
tog	together
tr	treble
trtr	triple treble
WS	wrong side
yd	yard(s)
yo	yarn over hook

* [ ] Repeat instructions after asterisk, between asterisks, or inside brackets as many times as instructed.

Your first crochet swatches

Whatever you crochet, it is important to take pride in your work and to ensure that it looks as good as it possibly can. Do not rush your crochet even when learning, and take time to make sure the work is as neat as you can make it. This will give you a sense of pride in your skills, and confidence to continue the craft and pick up more and more techniques.

As you follow the Workshops in this book, you will be making swatches to practice stitches and learn techniques. Be sure to keep the swatches you make and label them with the stitch name and the yarn and hook used. These are good references for future work and will become the basis of an interesting history of your personal adventures in crochet.

Pin your practicing swatches to a pinboard on the wall and watch your progress! Step back and see which stitches you prefer. Your personal crochet fabric favorites may become the smooth, simple stylish textures of the basic stitches, the interesting effects of highly textured stitches, elegant crochet lace, or eyecatching colorwork!

Understanding crochet gauge

Making swatches will become second nature as you learn the simple techniques of crochet, so you shouldn't be put off when eventually you need to make a "gauge" swatch when following you first crochet pattern. This swatch is made so that you can check the size of the your stitches before embarking on a project. It is also provides a good opportunity to test the yarn and feel of the crochet fabric.

Some people crochet loosely, some tightly and some in between, so there is no guarantee that they will achieve the same stitch size (gauge) as the designer of the crochet pattern they are following

while using the same hook size. How tightly or loosely you crochet usually depends on your "yarn tension," in other words, how tightly or loosely you let the yarn flow through your fingers. There is no "correct" or "incorrect" yarn tension; it is just a personal way of working. But you do need to work your stitches to the same size as those of the designer of a pattern so that your crochet ends up the right size.

The size of your finished crochet may not matter that much for a scarf, coasters, or a throw, for example, but it is essential for a garment. For this reason, the gauge you need to achieve is always given with the crochet pattern. You cannot change your crochet style to achieve the right stitch size, so instead you change your hook size if necessary.

To test your stitch size (the gauge) make a swatch about 5in (13cm) square using the yarn, hook size and crochet stitch specified in the pattern. (The pattern will tell you which stitch to use and it is usually the stitch that will be used in the pattern.)

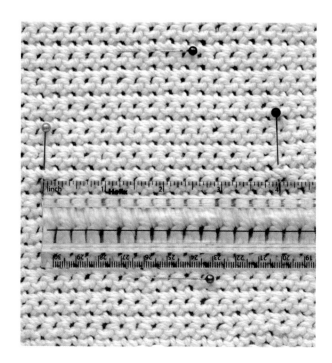

Smooth out your finished swatch on a flat surface and measure how many stitches and rows you have achieved to 4in (10cm).

If you have the same number of stitches and rows to 4in (10cm) as specified in the pattern, you can go ahead and work the project in the recommended hook size. If, however, you have too many stitches and rows, try again using a bigger hook size; if too few, use a smaller hook size.

You will be glad you took the time to check which hook size is right for you, when your new sweater fits you like a glove!

Blocking your crochet

The time and trouble you put into sewing together crochet pieces will make all the difference; it is just as important as making the crochet fabric itself. And the key to successful seams is well-blocked pieces. Blocking involves smoothing out and easing your crochet into the correct size and shape. Blocking is

also important for your learning swatches, as good blocking will really bring out the best in your work!

Before attempting to block any piece of crochet, look at the yarn label. If you are allowed to press the yarn (which you can most natural fibers), take note of how hot the iron can be.

The easiest way to block crochet is to pin it out to the correct size and shape, wrong side up, on a suitable padded surface (an ironing board is good), lay a clean damp cloth over it, and press it lightly. Use as many pins as you need along the edge to keep the edges straight and even, usually about one pin every 4–6cm (1½–2½in). Along shaped edges, such as those on edgings or many-sided motifs, you will need to put a pin at each "point" or corner along the edge.

Do not put the full weight of the iron on your crochet and do not drag it across the crochet, instead lift it to move it to other areas of the work. Let the crochet dry completely before removing the pins.

If your yarn label says that you cannot press it, or if the stitch has a very raised effect, then you can "wet" block instead. Pin the piece out as explained before and then either spray it with a fine mist of water or lay a clean damp cloth over it. Then leave it to dry completely.

Care of crochet

The most important tip for the care of your crochet is to keep the yarn label in a safe place! Refer to the label for washing or dry cleaning instructions. As with knitting, you should not wring out water when washing and rinsing, but instead gently squeeze water out. And always dry your crochet flat and out of direct sunlight to avoid damaging the fibers.

workshop

one

Getting to grips with crochet

The first step in crochet is to learn how to hold the hook and the yarn. There is no real right or wrong method, but the ones shown here are commonly used, and effective. Try them out when you begin making your first crochet stitches. With practice, you will find comfortable positions for the hook and yarn that will enable you to wrap the yarn around the hook easily. The aim is to make even stitches in a continuous, free-flowing motion.

Holding the hook

Pencil grip

There are two main ways of holding the crochet hook. The simplest way to remember them is to think of how you hold either a pencil or a knife. Some people find that the "knife grip" gives them more control, while others feel that the "pencil grip" allows for more fluidity of movement. It doesn't matter which one you use, so try both and see which one feels most comfortable. As you become more experienced, you may find that you adjust your grip slightly from the methods shown here.

Knife grip

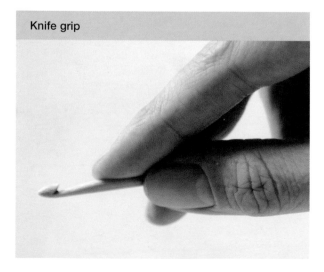

Troubleshooting tips

- You can learn to crochet with any hook size or yarn weight, but a good combination for a beginner is a size G-6 (4mm) crochet hook and either Rowan *Handknit Cotton* or *Pure Wool DK*.

- Don't grip the hook too tightly. Your hand should feel relaxed. If you experience difficulty with holding the hook, try a lighter or heavier hook, or one with a broad handle.

Holding the yarn

In order to create even stitches, you need to maintain an even tension on the yarn. This means the yarn needs to flow easily from the ball but with enough tension on it for the hook to be able to pick it up easily. To do this, you wind the yarn around your fingers so that you can hold it firmly and at the same time release it slowly.

Two ways of achieving a good yarn tension are shown here, although, in practice, you will probably find your own working method.

Method 1
Pass the working end (the ball end) of the yarn between the little finger and third finger of your left hand (if you are right handed), and then take it behind the third and middle fingers and over your index finger, as shown.

Method 2
Loop the working end of the yarn loosely around the little finger of your left hand, and then take it over your third finger, behind your middle finger and over your index finger, as shown.

Controlling the loop on the hook
Whichever method for holding the yarn you choose, you will need to control the crochet loop with the same hand that holds the yarn. When making your very first chain stitches on the following pages, hold the tail end of the yarn firmly between your left thumb and index finger, or thumb and middle finger. This enables you to control the position of the loop on the hook as the hook moves in and out of it.

The hook (held in your right hand) should be no more than about 1–2 inches (3–5cm) from your left index finger when you are crocheting.

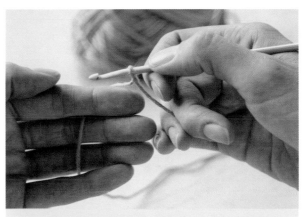
Tensioning the yarn—method 1

Tensioning the yarn—method 2

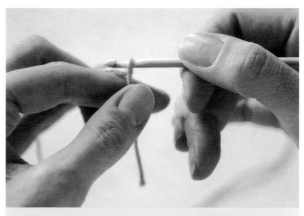
Holding the yarn tail to control the loop position

Making a slip knot

To start any piece of crochet, you need to make the first loop on the hook. This loop is called the *slip knot*.

1 Hold the tail from the ball of yarn in your left hand and drape the yarn clockwise over the top of it, to form a circular loop as shown.

2 Holding the loop between your left thumb and index finger, insert the crochet hook through the center of the loop from front to back.

3 Catch the ball end of the yarn with the lip of the hook and then pull the hook back through the center of the loop, drawing the yarn with it.

4 Pull both ends of the yarn until the knot below the hook is closed up. Then tighten the loop on the hook by pulling the ball end of the yarn only; the knot should be close to the hook but not touching it. If the loop is too tight, it will be difficult to pull the hook through it to make the following stitches. Try making the slip knot a few more times. Once you can do it easily, you are ready to continue the workshop.

Forming a circular loop of yarn

Inserting the hook through the loop

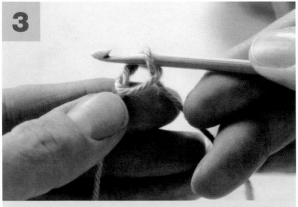

Pulling the ball end of the yarn through the loop

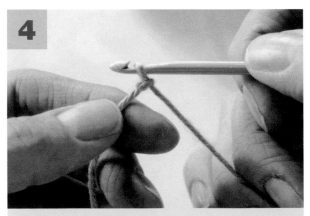

Tightening the slip knot on the hook

Learning the basic stitches

One of the joys of crochet is that you need master only a few very simple stitches in order to be able to produce a vast range of stylish, beautifully textured fabrics.

Generally speaking, the short basic stitches—slip stitch, single crochet, and half double crochet—create dense, firm textures, while the taller stitches, such as double crochet, treble crochet, and double treble crochet create an airier, more flexible fabric.

The swatches below are the commonly used basic stitches from the shortest (slip stitch) to the tallest (double treble). Learn them in the order they appear in the book and take your time with each one. Use the hook and yarn recommended in the tip box on page 18.

Slip stitch

Single crochet

Half double crochet

Double crochet

Treble crochet

Double treble crochet

Foundation chain

Crochet fabrics begin with what is called a foundation chain. It is made up of a series of identical crochet stitches, called *chains*. A crochet chain stitch is abbreviated in patterns as *ch*.

1 Make a slip knot on the hook as explained on page 20, and hold the yarn, hook, and slip knot as explained on pages 18 and 19.

2 Catch the ball end of the yarn with the hook, so that it wraps the yarn counterclockwise around it. (This is called "yarn over hook" and is abbreviated as *yo*.)

3 Draw the hook and its wrapped yarn back toward the loop on the hook...

4 ...and pull the yarn through to make a new loop on the hook. You have just made one chain.

5 Firmly holding the stitches below the hook, repeat Steps 2–4 until you have made about 20 chains. Then start over and make a new slip knot and another foundation chain. Continue until the movements feel easy and fluid and the chain stitches are even.

Troubleshooting tips

- Always make the chains for a foundation chain loosely so it will be easy to work the first row of stitches into them.

- To make even chain stitches, move the fingers holding the chain up toward the hook after every two or three stitches.

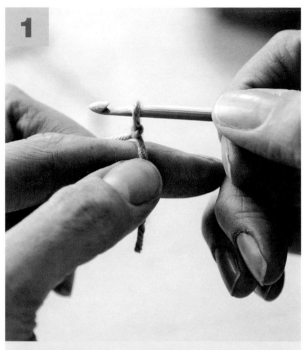

Holding the crochet slip knot in position

...and through the loop to make a new chain

2

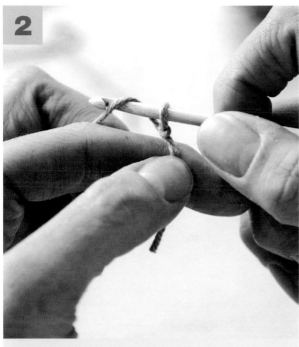

Catching the yarn with the hook

3

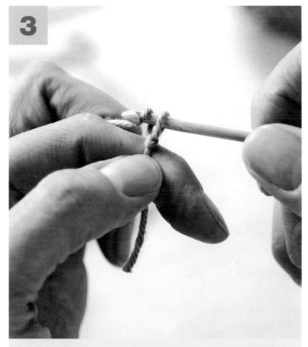

Drawing the yarn toward the loop on the hook...

5

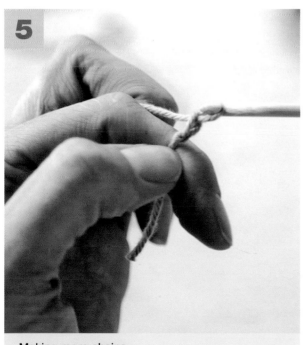

Making more chains

The completed foundation chain. These chains form the base for your subsequent stitches.

Abbreviation = ch   Symbol = ⌒ (see page 13)

Uses for the basic stitches

Used on its own, each basic stitch creates a different type of fabric. The short stitches create a denser, tighter fabric; the taller ones an open-textured and airier one. The taller the stitch, the quicker it is to work, and the faster the crochet fabric will grow.

- **Slip stitch**, the shortest stitch, is rarely used to create a solid fabric. However, it is ideal for joining one part of the crochet to another, or when you need to work an almost invisible stitch to move your crochet hook along to another point on the fabric. It can also be worked along an edge to minimize stretching.

- **Single crochet** is taller than slip stitch and creates a firm, dense fabric useful for making warm sweaters and items that require a sculptural shape, such as containers, hats, and toys. It is also often used for firm, narrow edgings on crocheted and knitted fabrics.

- **Half double crochet** creates a fairly dense fabric much like single crochet, but a slightly less firm and more flexible one. It is often used on its own for garments and in conjunction with other stitches to form textured stitch patterns (see pages 106–115).

- **Double crochet**, **treble crochet,** and **double treble crochet** create softer, more openwork fabrics. They are ideal used on their own for scarves and shawls, and used in conjunction with other stitches to form lace and afghan motif patterns.

Slip stitch

A crochet slip stitch is the shortest of the basic crochet stitches. It is abbreviated as *sl st*. Because slip stitch is rarely used on its own to make a fabric, it is only necessary to learn how to work it along a foundation chain for the time being. Learning it is good practice for working into the foundation chain. If you want to try working it in rows, you can come back to it later.

1 Make a foundation chain of the desired length—about 20 chains is sufficient. You will be working the first stitch into the **second** chain from the hook (see arrow). The loop on the hook does not count as part of the chain, so count only the chains next to the hook when figuring out which chain to work into first.

2 Holding the foundation chain between the thumb and index finger of the yarn hand, insert the hook through the chain under one top loop of the second chain from the hook. Catch the ball end of the yarn with the hook so that it wraps the yarn counterclockwise around it.

3 Draw the yarn around the hook through the chain and then through the loop on the hook. You have just made your first slip stitch. Work one slip stitch into each remaining chain of the foundation chain in the same way.

Troubleshooting tip

If the stitches of your foundation chain are too tight to work into easily, even though you tried to work them loosely, use a hook one size larger for it and revert to the smaller hook to work the rest of the crochet fabric.

1

Making your foundation chain

2

Working into the second chain from the hook

3

Completing the first slip stitch

The completed row of slip stitches. You will be using slip stitches later when working crochet in the round and for decreases.

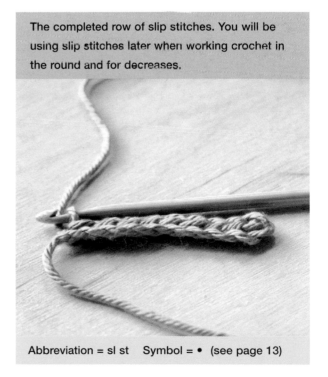

Abbreviation = sl st   Symbol = • (see page 13)

Making your foundation chain

Single crochet

Once you have practiced working slip stitches on a foundation chain a few times (see pages 24–25), you can move on to single crochet. Do not attempt the other basic stitches until you are confident that you have completely mastered single crochet. In patterns, single crochet is abbreviated as *sc*.

1 Make a foundation chain of the desired length— about 20 chains is sufficient. You will be working the first stitch into the **second** chain from the hook (see arrow) as you did for slip stitch.

2 Holding the foundation chain as shown, insert the hook into the second chain from the hook.

3 Catch the yarn with the hook and wrap it around the hook (*yo*) in the usual way.

4 Draw the yarn through the chain, so that there are now two loops on the hook.

5 Wrap the yarn around the hook again.

6 Draw the yarn through both loops on the hook to complete the stitch. Work one single crochet into each chain that remains in the same way.

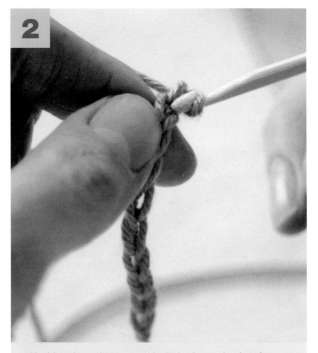

Working into the second chain from the hook

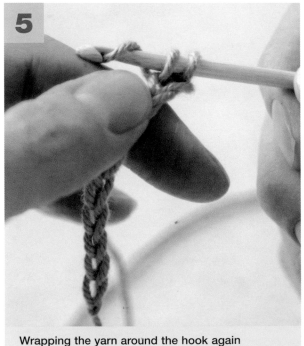

Wrapping the yarn around the hook again

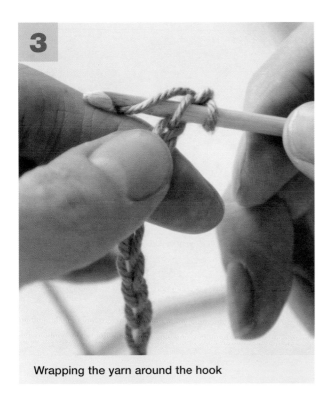

Wrapping the yarn around the hook

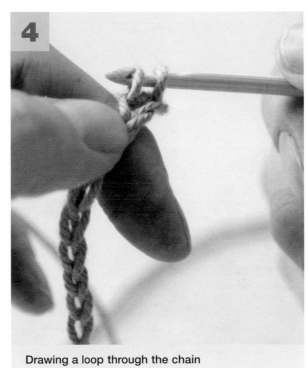

Drawing a loop through the chain

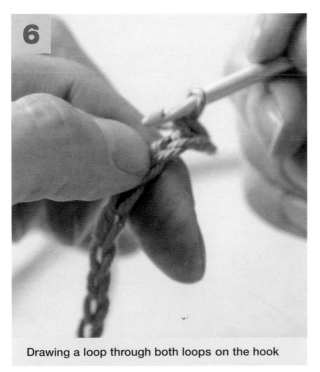

Drawing a loop through both loops on the hook

The completed row of single crochet. You are now ready to crochet the second row of single crochet as explained on the next page.

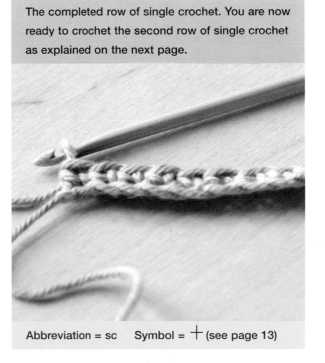

Abbreviation = sc   Symbol = + (see page 13)

Working the second row of sc

1 After completing the first row of single crochet stitches along the foundation chain, turn your crochet so that the yarn is now at the right edge of the work. To begin the second row of single crochet, first work one chain (known as a *turning chain*—see opposite). If you look at the top of the stitches, you can see that they form V-shapes—the top of the crochet is turned in this picture so you can see them clearly. To begin the first stitch, insert the hook into the top of the first stitch of the previous row, making sure that it passes UNDER BOTH SIDES of the V-shape as shown. Then complete the first single crochet in the usual way.

2 Work one single crochet into the top of each of the remaining stitches of the previous row in the same way to complete the first row. Work the following rows in the same way as the second row. Continue practicing rows of single crochet until you feel you are doing it automatically and fluidly.

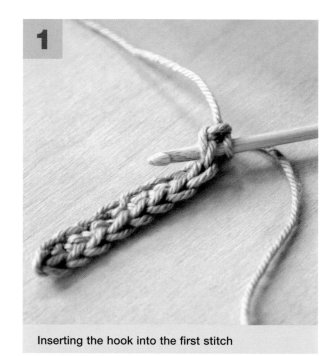

Inserting the hook into the first stitch

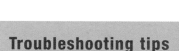

Troubleshooting tips

- After working the row of single crochet into your foundation chain, count the number of single crochet stitches you have. After the second row, count your stitches again—you should have the same number as the first row. Because it is easy to skip the edge stitches when learning, count again a few rows later.

- Relax and enjoy the process of learning single crochet. The first two rows may seem difficult but you will soon be surprised how easy it is!

Working one single crochet into each stitch

Working turning chains

When working the basic stitches, at the beginning of the second row and all following rows of the basic stitches you need to make what is known as the *turning chain* (abbreviated as *t-ch*). The turning chain consists of one or more chain stitches, and it is necessary in order to bring the work up level with the top of the following stitches in the row you are about to work.

How many chains to work

Failing to make a turning chain of the right height for the particular stitch you are working will create uneven edges along the sides of the crochet fabric. The taller the stitch, the taller the turning chain needs to be. Here is a list of the basic stitches and how many chains to work for the turning chain at the start of the row.

Slip stitch	1 chain
Single crochet	1 chain
Half double crochet	2 chains
Double crochet	3 chains
Treble crochet	4 chains
Double treble crochet	5 chains

When to work the turning chain

Because the turning chain is part of the row you are about to begin, it is best to work it at the start of the row you are about to begin. Traditionally, however, it was often worked at the end of the previous row and before the crochet work was turned (hence its name). It makes no difference to the appearance of the work whether you make the chains before or after you turn your work, but it is easiest to get used to working with one method or the other.

Does the turning chain count as a stitch?

On the shorter stitches—slip stitch, single crochet, and half double crochet—after working the turning chain at the beginning of a row, you work the first stitch into the first stitch of the previous row (see the symbols below). For these stitches, the turning chain is NOT usually counted as a stitch in its own right.

For double crochet, treble crochet, and the taller stitches, the turning chain counts as the first stitch in the row, so you skip the first stitch in the previous row and work your first stitch into the next stitch. If the turning is counted as a stitch, remember to work into the top of it at the end of the row as you would any other stitch. The stitch symbols below show the turning chains and stitch positions for single and double crochet very clearly.

Rows of single crochet in symbols

Rows of double crochet in symbols

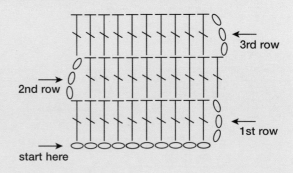

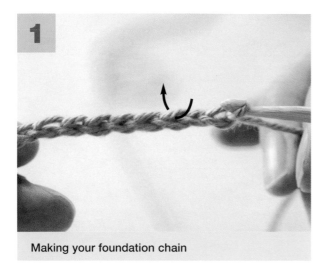

Making your foundation chain

Wrapping the yarn once around the hook

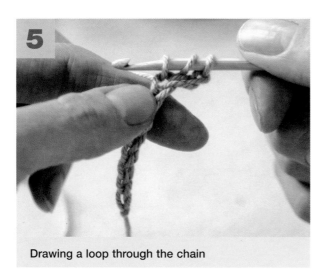

Drawing a loop through the chain

Wrapping the yarn around the hook once more

Half double crochet

Once you have mastered single crochet and can work it without looking at the step-by-step instructions, you could make many crochet designs without ever learning any more stitches. However, if you take a little more time and learn three more basic stitches, you will be able to follow any crochet pattern on offer!

The next stitch to learn is half double crochet. It is abbreviated as *hdc* in patterns.

1 Make a foundation chain of the desired length. You will be working the first stitch into the **third** chain from the hook (see arrow).

2 To begin the first stitch, first catch the yarn with the hook and wrap it around the hook in the usual way.

3 Insert the hook into the third chain from the hook.

4 Wrap the yarn around the hook again.

Working into the third chain from the hook

Wrapping the yarn around the hook again

Drawing a loop through all three loops on the hook

5 Draw the yarn through the chain so that there are now three loops on the hook.

6 Wrap the yarn around the hook again.

7 Draw the yarn through all three loops on the hook to complete the first half double crochet. Work one half double crochet into each chain that remains in the same way.

The completed row of half double crochet. You are now ready to crochet the second row of half double crochet as explained on the next page.

Abbreviation = hdc   Symbol = ⊤ (see page 13)

Working the second row of hdc

1 After completing the first row of half double crochet along the foundation chain, turn your crochet so that the yarn is now at the right edge of the work. To begin the second row of half double crochet, first work two chains for the turning chain (see page 29).

2 Begin the first half double crochet in the usual way, by wrapping the yarn once around the hook (*yo*). Then insert the hook into the top of the first stitch of the previous row, making sure that it passes UNDER BOTH SIDES of the V-shape at the top of the stitch. Complete the half double crochet in the usual way. Work one half double crochet into the top of each of the remaining stitches of the previous row. Continue practicing rows of half double crochet, working the following rows in the same way as the second row. Once you can work the stitch without referring to the Steps, you are ready to learn your next stitch.

Working two chains for the turning chain

Troubleshooting tip

There is very little difference between single crochet and half double crochet—just the extra "yo" (yarn over hook) before each stitch is begun. Because you are wrapping the yarn around the hook more times with this stitch, now is the time to concentrate on the yarn-wrapping motion. You may already have noticed that when you catch the yarn with the hook, your yarn-holding hand tends to thrust the yarn forward to facilitate the wrapping motion—this is natural. If you aren't already doing this, try it! It will speed up your work.

Working one half double crochet into each stitch

Different yarns and hooks

So far, all the examples of crochet shown in this workshop have used one yarn (Rowan *Handknit Cotton*) and one hook size—a size G-6 (4mm) hook. This particular combination makes stitches that are easy to see clearly for photography purposes, but your own crochet may look very different depending on the yarn and hook size chosen.

Denser or lacier effects can be achieved by varying the hook size, and heavier weight yarns will grow more quickly on bigger hooks. Shown here are five examples worked in different yarns, with different hooks sizes.

If you want to try something new before going on to learn more stitches, have some fun working the stitches you already know using different hook sizes and various yarn scraps you have at hand. There are no rules about which hook size to use with which yarn. It all depends on the type of fabric you want to create. Experiment with the same yarn using different hook sizes to see the difference it makes to the texture of the crochet.

Double crochet worked with Rowan *Cotton Glace* and a size C-2 (2.5mm) hook

Double crochet worked with Rowan *RYC Silk Wool DK* and a size E-4 (3.5mm) hook

Half double crochet worked with Rowan *Handknit Cotton* and a size E-4 (3.5mm) hook

Half double crochet worked with Rowan *Kidsilk Haze* and a size 7 (4.5mm) hook

Single crochet worked with Rowan *Big Wool* and a size L-11 (8mm) hook

Making your foundation chain

Wrapping the yarn once around the hook

Double crochet

If you have been experimenting with different yarns and hook sizes after learning half double crochet, be sure to go back to the recommended yarn and hook size (see page 18) when trying out your next stitch—double crochet. This combination will make it as easy as possible for you to learn the stitches.

Double crochet is slightly taller than half double crochet but is made in a very similar way. In patterns, double crochet is abbreviated as *dc*.

1 Make a foundation chain of the desired length. For double crochet, you will be working the first stitch into the **fourth** chain from the hook (see arrow).

2 Wrap the yarn once around the hook in the usual way.

3 Insert the hook into the fourth chain from the hook.

4 Wrap the yarn around the hook again.

5 Draw the yarn through the chain. There are now three loops on the hook.

6 Wrap the yarn around the hook once more.

7 Pull the hook through the first two loops on the hook. There are now two loops on the hook.

(continued on page 36)

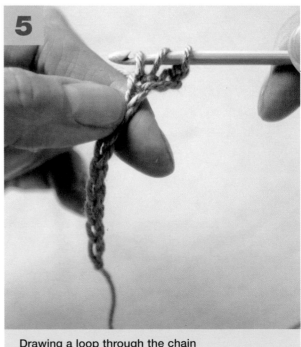

Drawing a loop through the chain

3

Working into the fourth chain from the hook

4

Wrapping the yarn around the hook again

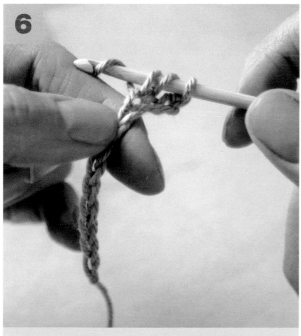

6

Wrapping the yarn around the hook again

7

Drawing a loop through the first two loops

Wrapping the yarn around the hook once more

Drawing a loop through the last two loops

8 Wrap the yarn around the hook once more.

9 Draw a loop through the remaining two loops on the hook to complete the first double crochet. One loop remains on the hook. Work one double crochet into each of the remaining chains in the same way.

Troubleshooting tip

Make sure you can work double crochet with ease before attempting the second row.

The completed row of double crochet. You are now ready to crochet the second row of double crochet as explained on the next page.

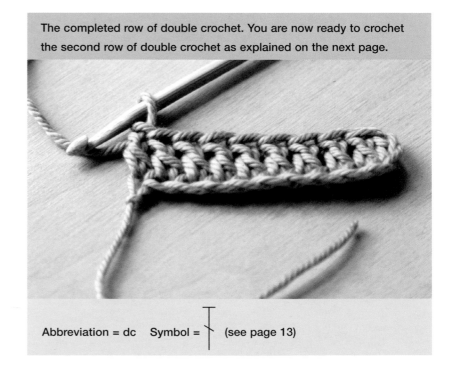

Abbreviation = dc   Symbol = (see page 13)

Working the second row of dc

1 After completing the first row of double crochet along the foundation chain, turn your work so that the yarn is now at the right edge of the crochet. Start the second row by making three chains for the turning chain (see page 29). This turning chain counts as the first stitch of the second row (and of all following rows).

2 Skip the first stitch on the previous row and work the first double into the top of the SECOND stitch. Work one double into the top of each of the remaining doubles of the previous row. Work the last double into the third of the three free chains at the end (these are the three chains skipped in the foundation chain at the beginning of of the first row).

Troubleshooting tip

All the following rows of double crochet are worked in the same way as the second row. Always remember to work the last double crochet of each row into the top (the third chain) of the turning chain in the previous row.

Working three chains for the turning chain

Working one double crochet into each stitch

Making your foundation chain

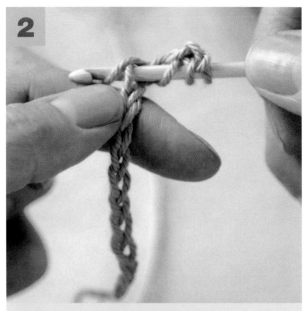

Working into the fifth chain from the hook

Treble crochet

Once you have learned this stitch you will be able to pick up double trebles on your own. They are worked in the same way except that each one is begun with three wraps around the hook, the first stitch is worked into the sixth chain from the hook, and it requires five chains for the turning chain instead of four. Try out double trebles (*tr*) first, then double trebles (*dtr*).

1 Make a foundation chain of the required length. You will be working the first stitch into the **fifth** chain from the hook (see arrow).

2 Wrap the yarn twice around the hook, then insert the hook into the fifth chain from the hook and wrap the yarn around the hook again.

3 Draw a loop through the chain. There are four loops on the hook. *Wrap the yarn around the hook...

4 ...and draw a loop through the first two loops on the hook.* Repeat from * to * until there is only one loop left on the hook. This completes the first stitch. Work one stitch into each remaining chain in the same way.

...and drawing a loop through two loops at a time until one loop remains on the hook

Wrapping the yarn around the hook again...

The completed row of treble crochet. You are now ready to crochet the second row of treble crochet as explained right.

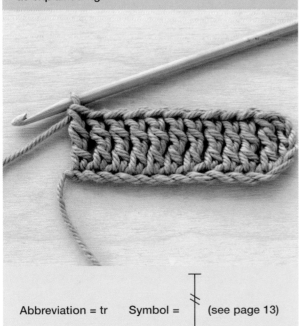

Abbreviation = tr   Symbol = (see page 13)

Working the second row of tr

1 At the beginning of the second row, make four chains for the turning chain, which counts as the first stitch of the second and of all following rows.

2 Complete the second row as for double crochet, but work the last treble into the fourth of the four free chains at the end.

Working four chains for the turning chain

Working one treble into each stitch

Fastening off

At this stage in the workshop you may already have figured out how easy it is to fasten off your crochet because at the end of each row all you have on your hook is one remaining loop. Follow these simple steps for a few useful tips.

1 Cut the yarn, leaving a yarn tail about 4–6in (10–15cm) long—you need a length long enough to thread onto a blunt-ended yarn needle. Then wrap the yarn tail around the hook.

2 Pull the yarn through the loop on the hook and pull the tail of yarn to tighten the loop against the end of the crocheted piece. Thread the yarn tail onto a blunt-ended yarn needle and darn it into the wrong side of the crochet. Do the same with the yarn tail at the end of the foundation chain.

Troubleshooting tips

- Now that you can work double crochet, treble crochet, and double treble crochet with relative ease, why not turn back to page 33 and experiment with using different yarns and hook sizes for these tall stitches? You can make tiny square swatches and label them for future reference. Alternatively, turn to page 43 and practice your stitches by making practical cotton coasters.

- If you have had difficulty with any of the lessons in Workshop One, don't despair. Ask a friend who can crochet for help. They may be able to quickly identify where you are going wrong and find a simple solution for you.

Wrapping the yarn tail around the hook

Pulling the yarn tail to tighten the loop

Where to insert your hook

So far, in this workshop you have learned to work the individual basic stitches on their own in rows. However, with the skills you now have you will also be able to work a different stitch in each row if you follow the simple instructions for the little coaster project on page 43. In later workshops some of the lessons will focus on mixing the stitches together in the same row to make textured or lace patterns.

The crochet stitch dissected

Before going on to the following workshops, have a closer look at the basic stitches. When you first start to crochet you may find it hard to work out exactly where to insert your hook. The illustration below identifies the different parts of a chain and a basic stitch. These are the parts that you will need to be able to locate when you start to learn how to work a variety of crochet stitch patterns.

Parts of a chain

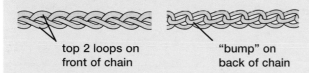

top 2 loops on
front of chain

"bump" on
back of chain

Parts of a stitch

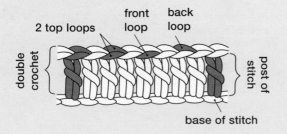

2 top loops   front
loop   back
loop

double
crochet   post
of
stitch

base of stitch

Working into a chain

When you learn to work basic stitches into the foundation chain, it is easiest to work into only one loop of a chain—one of the two top loops. Once you become more proficient, try working into the chain differently to see if you prefer the effect. Working stitches into both top loops or into only the back "bump" produces very neat edges.

Working into a stitch

Whenever a crochet pattern tells you to work a basic stitch, always insert your hook under both the top two loops of the stitch (under the V-shape) as you have already learned (see below). But in later workshops you will discover that you can work into other parts of the stitch as well, to create a vast range of different textures and lace patterns.

A stitch can also be worked into the front or back loop only, around the post, into the space between two stitches, and even into a stitch two rows (or more) below. This is what makes crochet so versatile!

Working into different parts of a stitch

working into
top of stitch
in usual way
(under 2 loops)   working
into front
loop only   working into
back loop only

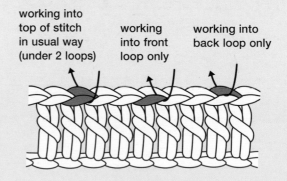

project **one**

Four-stitch coaster

This very simple first project uses just four basic stitches—single, half double, double, and treble crochet. It offers you the opportunity to practice your stitches and make something you can use. It also gives you your first chance to follow a written out crochet pattern as well as a pattern in symbols (see page 13). The symbol instructions will help you follow the written pattern and vice versa.

Size
The finished coaster measures approximately 4½in (11.5cm) by 4½in (11.5cm).

What you need
One 1¾oz/50g ball of Rowan *Handknit Cotton* in desired color, or scraps of same yarn in several colors
size G-6 (4mm) crochet hook
Note: One ball is enough for 3 to 4 coasters.

Gauge
Working to an exact stitch size, or gauge (see page 14), to obtain an exact size of coaster is not important for this project; the aim is to make a squarish coaster.

Abbreviations and symbols
See page 13.

Written instructions
Using size G-6 (4mm) hook, ch 18 (for the foundation chain).
Row 1 1 sc in 2nd ch from hook, 1 sc in each of remaining ch, turn. *17 sc.*
Row 2 Ch 2 (does NOT count as first st), 1 hdc in each sc to end, turn.

Row 3 Ch 1, (does NOT count as first st), 1 sc in each hdc to end, turn.
Row 4 Ch 4 (counts as first tr), skip first sc, *1 tr in next sc; rep from * to end, turn.
Row 5 Ch 1 (does NOT count as first st), 1 sc in each tr to end, 1 sc in 4th of 4-ch, turn.
Row 6 Ch 3 (counts as first dc), skip first sc, *1 dc in next sc; rep from * to end, turn.
Row 7 Ch 2 (does NOT count as first st), 1 hdc in each dc to end, 1 hdc in 3rd of 3-ch, turn.
Row 8 Ch 3 (counts as first dc), skip first hdc, *1 dc in next hdc; rep from * to end, turn.
Row 9 Ch 1 (does NOT count as first st), 1 sc in each dc to end, 1 sc in 3rd of 3-ch, turn.
Rows 10 and 11 Rep rows 4 and 5.
Rows 12 and 13 Rep rows 2 and 3. Fasten off.

Symbol instructions

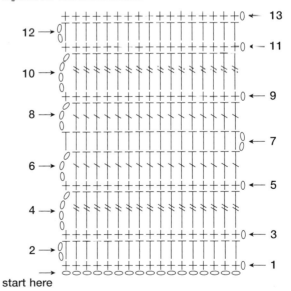

Finishing
Darn in any yarn ends.
Block and press (see page 15).

workshop
two

Working stripes

Once you learn how to join in a new yarn, you can not only start a new ball of yarn, but you can also begin to introduce different colors into your crochet, in a series of simple row-by-row stripes. Follow the steps for joining in a new color given here, and then make the scarf on pages 50 and 51 to experiment with your new skills. In the rest of Workshop Two you will discover how to add simple edgings and join pieces of crochet together.

Joining in a new yarn

You can join in a new color for stripes either at the end of a row or near the end of the row (see right and pages 48–49). Both these methods can also be used to join in a new ball of yarn of the same color (see tips below). The steps show single crochet stripes, but the principle is the same for all the basic stitches.

Troubleshooting tips

- It is easiest to join in a new ball of yarn at the end of a row rather than in the middle. When you see that you might not have enough yarn left to work another row, change to the new ball following one of the methods used for changing to a new color. These techniques provide a neat, secure changeover and eliminate the need to darn in loose ends.

- If you do have any loose yarn ends when the crochet is complete, thread each one onto a blunt-ended yarn needle and weave it through the stitches on the wrong side of the work. On stripes, weave the end into a matching color.

Joining in a new color at the end of the row

1 Work to the last stitch of the row. Then work the last stitch up to the point where two loops remain on the hook. Cut the yarn, leaving a 2in (5cm) tail.

2 Lay the end of the new yarn over the hook, leaving a tail about 4in (10cm) long.

3 Draw the new yarn through both loops on the hook to complete the last stitch. Pull the ends of both the old and the new yarns to tighten the loop on the hook.

4 Turn the work and work the turning chain with the new color. You can now see why you changed to the new color with the last "yo" of the last stitch of the previous row—the turning chain is now in the correct color for the start of the new stripe.

5 Lay the cut ends of both the old and the new yarns along the top edge of the crochet and work the first stitch over them.

6 Work at least four more stitches over the yarn ends so that they are firmly secured. Then complete the row without working over the yarn ends any more. Trim off the ends of the yarn tails close to the work.

1

Working up to the last "yo" of the last stitch

2

Laying the new color over the hook

3

Pulling the new color through both loops

4

Working the turning chain with the new color

5

Working the first stitch over the yarn ends

6

Working at least four more stitches over the ends

Joining in a new color near the end of a row

The main advantages of this method are that you only have to deal with one end of yarn at a time and the ends are a little more secure. However, if the yarn colors are highly contrasting, the new color may be visible in the last few stitches of the row.

1 At least six stitches before the end of the row, lay the end of the new yarn along the top of the work. Complete the row, working over the new yarn.

2 On the last stitch of the row, join in the new yarn as before, using it for the last "yo" of the row. Turn the crochet and work the turning chain with the new color.

3 Cut the old yarn leaving a 2in (5cm) tail. Lay this tail along the top of the work and begin working over it.

4 Work at least six stitches over the old yarn end.

Laying new yarn across the top of the crochet

Half double crochet stripes

When working half double crochet stripes, change to the new color as for single crochet—with the last "yo" of the row. In this case there will be three loops left on the hook when you change colors.

Working in the first two stitches over the end

2

Working the turning chain with the new color

4

Working at least four more stitches over the end

Two-row stripes

If your stripes are only two rows deep and you are using only two colors, there is no need to cut the working yarn and join in the new yarn every time you change color. Instead, drop the old color at the side of the work, and when you need it again simply pick it up and begin working with it. This method forms short, neat strands of yarn along one side of the crochet (see below) and is known as "stranding." Change to the new color with the last "yo" of the last row of the stripe in the usual way, but be careful not to pull the new yarn too tightly or the work may pucker.

This technique is only suitable for two-row stripes, however. If you crochet one or three rows before changing yarn, the yarn that you want to use will be at the opposite edge of the work. Strands carried up the side of four-row stripes (or taller ones) will be too long and could easily be snagged. In these cases, cut the old yarn when introducing the new color and work over the ends as explained left and on pages 46–47.

Striped mixed-yarn scarf

This striped scarf is very easy to make. It is enhanced by the combination of different yarn textures as well as by the use of three different stitches—single, double, and treble crochet. The stripes on the scarf run the length of the scarf. If you want a longer scarf, simply work a longer foundation chain when starting.

Try out the methods you learned for joining in new colors by changing to the new color with the last "yo" of the last stitch of the previous row and working over the yarn ends (see pages 46–49).

Size
The finished scarf measures approximately 5½in (14cm) wide by 55½in (141cm) long, excluding tassels.

What you need
Rowan *RYC Cashcotton DK* in one color as follows:

A Cashew (619)   1 x 1¾oz/50g ball

Rowan *Kidsilk Haze* in three colors as follows:

B Pearl (590)   1 x ⅞oz/25g ball
C Heavenly (592)   1 x ⅞oz/25g ball
D Dewberry (600)   1 x ⅞oz/25g ball
E Meadow (581)   1 x ⅞oz/25g ball

Size 7 (4.5mm) crochet hook
Size G-6 (4mm) crochet hook

Abbreviations
See page 13.

Gauge
14 sts and 8 rows to 4in (10cm) measured over patt using size G-6 (4mm) hook *or size necessary to obtain correct gauge*.

Special yarn note
Use two strands together of yarns B, C, D, and E (Rowan *Kidsilk Haze*).

Scarf
Using size 7 (4.5mm) hook and A, ch 200.
Change to size G-6 (4mm) hook.
Row 1 1 dc in 4th ch from hook, 1 dc in each of remaining ch, turn. *198 sts.*
Cutting off and joining in new yarns as required, cont in stripes as follows:
Row 2 Using B, ch 3 (counts as first dc), skip first dc, *1 dc in next dc; rep from * to end, 1 dc in 3rd of 3-ch, turn.
Row 3 Using A, ch 1 (does NOT count as first st), 1 sc in each dc to end, 1 sc in 3rd of 3-ch, turn.
Row 4 Using D, ch 4 (counts as first tr), skip first sc, *1 tr in next sc; rep from * to end, turn.
Row 5 Using A, ch 1 (does NOT count as first st), 1 sc each tr to end, 1 sc in 4th of 4-ch, turn.
Row 6 Using B, ch 3 (counts as first dc), skip first sc, *1 dc in next sc; rep from * to end, turn.
Row 7 Using A, rep row 3.
Row 8 Using C, rep row 4.
Row 9 Using A, rep row 5.
Row 10 Using B, rep row 6.
Row 11 Using A, rep row 3.
Row 12 Using E, ch 1 (does NOT count as first st), 1 sc each sc to end, turn.
Row 13 Using A, rep row 12.
Row 14 Using B, rep row 6.
Row 15 Using A, rep row 2. Fasten off.

Finishing
Do not press. Darn in any remaining yarn ends.
Tassels
Make four tassels for each end of scarf and attach them, equally spaced, along the end. For each tassel, cut 10 lengths of A and 20 lengths of B, each 10in (25cm) long. Align lengths and fold them in half. Using a crochet hook, draw loop of strands at folded end through end of scarf, then pull cut ends through loop and pull to tighten.

Simple crochet edgings

Adding a simple crocheted edging is an easy way to provide an attractive finishing touch for any crochet project, from simple scarves to pillows and throws. This lesson shows you how to crochet a simple edging directly onto a finished piece—along the top and bottom of the piece and along the row-end side edges. After you learn more sophisticated stitch techniques in Workshop Four, you will be able to progress to the lacier edgings in Workshop Six.

Starting a crochet edging

The first thing you need to learn when working a crochet edging onto a finished piece of crochet is how to join on the edging yarn. You can do this by simply working a single slip stitch through the edge (see pages 24–25), but the technique shown is more secure. Whenever a crochet pattern tells you to "join" a yarn to a finished piece of crochet, use this method.

1 Using the edging yarn, make a slip knot on your hook (see page 20); then remove the hook. Hold this loop behind the beginning of the edge you will be working onto. Insert your crochet hook through the top of the first stitch on the edge of the finished piece of crochet and pull the slip knot through.

2 Begin working the first stitch of the edging in the usual way—usually the turning chain.

Pulling the slip knot through the first edge stitch

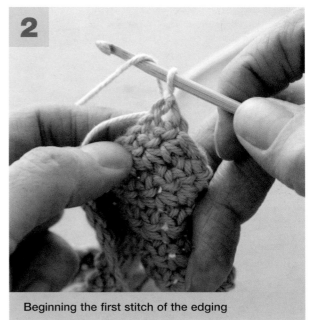

Beginning the first stitch of the edging

Single crochet edging

The simplest crochet edging of all is a single crochet edging. It creates a neat, subtle line of contrasting color along the edge of your crochet. A single row of single crochet is also often used to form the first row of more elaborate edgings.

Practice working this edging along the foundation-chain edge of a piece of crochet first; then along a row-end edge (see right). Using the same size hook you used for the finished crochet, join the edging yarn to the bottom of the first foundation chain stitch as explained on the previous page. After pulling the slip knot through the first stitch of the edge of the finished crochet, work one chain for the turning chain. Then work the first single crochet in the same stitch that you joined the slip knot to, working over the yarn tail of the edging yarn. Continue along the edge, working one single crochet into each stitch and covering the yarn tail as your proceed (see below). Fasten off after the last stitch.

Working a single crochet edging

Working along row ends

When your are working a single crochet edging along either the last row of your crochet or along the foundation-chain edge, it is easy to position the stitches because you are working one single crochet into each stitch on the finished piece.

Working along the sides—or row ends—of a finished piece is not as easy. If your instructions don't tell you how many stitches to work, space the stitches evenly along the row ends by eye and by trial and error. Begin by crocheting just a small section along the edge, and then take time to look at it critically to see if it looks right.

Faulty side edging
If you place the edging stitches too close together, the edge will splay out (see above). Stitches too far apart will pull in the edge.

Correct side edging
Evenly spaced stitches will keep the side edge of the crochet the same length it was before the edging was added.

Simple decorative edgings

There are many simple decorative edgings that you now have the skills to work directly onto your finished piece of crochet. Step-by-step instructions for a simple scallop edging are given here and several alternative simple edgings on pages 56–57.

The simple scallop edging gives you the opportunity to practice using more than one basic stitch in the same row. A combination of four stitches of different heights creates an attractive wavy edge.

Instructions within a crochet pattern for decorative edgings will have been carefully worked out so that the edging repeat perfectly fits the finished piece. But if you are working onto your own piece of crochet, you will have to count the number of stitches along your piece and calculate whether the the edging will fit it neatly and won't finish halfway through the motif repeat. It doesn't matter too much if you're left with only one or two stitches to work into at the end of the row; just work an extra slip stitch or two to complete the row. Alternatively, choose an edging with a smaller repeat.

Troubleshooting tips

- For an edging along the TOP ROW of your crochet, there is no need to join on the edging yarn with a slip knot. Just change to the edging yarn with the last "yo" of the last row, turn and begin the edging.

- To work a simple single crochet edging around the corner of a piece, work three stitches into the corner and continue along the next edge in the usual way. Working a decorative edging around a corner requires special instructions.

Working the first chain with the edging yarn

Working a simple scallop edging

This simple scallop edging is worked over a multiple of seven stitches plus one extra. Practice working it along the foundation-chain edge of a piece of crochet.

1 Join on the edging yarn by drawing a slip knot through the bottom of the first foundation chain (see page 52). Then work one chain to secure the slip knot.

2 *Work one single crochet in the next stitch, one half double crochet in the next stitch, and one double crochet in each of the next two stitches.

3 To decrease the scallop height, work one half double crochet in the next stitch, one single crochet in the next stitch, and one slip stitch in the next stitch.*

4 Repeat from * to * along the edge; then fasten off.

Increasing the height of the scallop

Deceasing the height of the scallop

Coming to the end of the second scallop

Small picot edging

Shell picot edging

Two-color picot edging

Fan scallop edging

Two-color afghan edging

Open shell edging

Simple edging patterns

Here are some additional crochet edging designs, worked in one or two colors. They have all been worked directly onto the last row of a crocheted fabric. If you like, you could also work them along the foundation-chain edge (or evenly spaced along a row-end side edge as explained on page 53).

Most of these edgings will fit an edge of any length as they are worked either over any number of stitches or over an odd number of stitches. For edgings that are worked over a specific multiple of stitches, make sure they will fit before beginning. Start each edging with a slip knot as explained on page 52.

Small picot edging

This edging is worked over any number of sts.
Row 1 (RS) With RS facing, join yarn to first st, ch 3, 1 sl st in same place as 3-ch, *work [1 sl st, ch 3, 1 sl st] all in next st; rep from * to end. Fasten off.

Shell picot edging

This edging is worked over an odd number of sts.
Row 1 (RS) With RS facing, join yarn to first st, ch 1, 1 sc in same place as 1-ch, *ch 3, 1 sc in same st as last sc, 1 sc in each of next 2 sc; rep from * to end. Fasten off.

Two-color picot edging

This edging is worked over a multiple of 3 sts plus 2 extra. It is worked with two colors: A and B.
Row 1 (WS) With WS facing and using A, join yarn to first st, ch 1, 1 sc in same place as 1-ch, 1 sc in each st to end, changing to B with last yo of last sc, turn.
Row 2 (RS) Using B, *ch 3, skip 1 sc, 1 sl st in each of next 2 sc; rep from *, omitting 2nd sl st at end of last repeat. Fasten off.

Fan scallop edging

This edging is worked over a multiple of 4 sts.
Row 1 (WS) With WS facing, join yarn to first st, ch 1, 1 sc in same place as 1-ch, 1 sc in each st to end, turn.
Row 2 (RS) *Skip 1 sc, 5 dc in next sc, skip 1 sc, 1 sl st in next sc; rep from * to end. Fasten off.

Two-color afghan edging

This edging is worked over an odd number of sts. It is worked with two colors: A and B.
Row 1 (RS) With RS facing and using A, join yarn to first st, ch 1, 1 sc in same place as 1-ch, 1 sc in each st to end. Fasten off.
(**Note:** Do not turn at end of rows, but rejoin new color at beg of each row with RS facing.)
Row 2 (RS) Using B, join yarn to first sc, ch 3, 1 dc into same place as 3-ch, *skip 1 sc, 2 dc in next sc; rep from * to end. Fasten off.
Row 3 (RS) Using A, join yarn to 3rd of 3-ch at beg of previous row, ch 3, *2 dc in space between next 2 dc; rep from * to end, 1 dc in last dc. Fasten off.
Row 4 (RS) Using B, join yarn to 3rd of 3-ch at beg of previous row, 1 sl st in next dc, *work [1 sl st, ch 3, 1 sl st] all in next dc, 1 sl st in next dc; rep from * to end. Fasten off.

Open shell edging

This edging is worked over an odd number of sts.
Row 1 (WS) With WS facing, join yarn to first st, ch 5, skip next st, 1 dc in next st, *ch 2, skip next st, 1 dc in next st; rep from * to end, turn.
Row 2 (RS) Ch 1, *5 sc in next 2-ch space (see page 78), 1 sl st in next dc; rep from * to last ch space, 5 sc in last ch space, 1 sl st in 3rd of 5-ch. Fasten off.

Crocheting edgings onto other fabrics

One of the many advantages of crochet is that you can work crochet edgings very easily directly onto knitting and loosely woven fabrics or jerseys, in exactly the same way you would work directly onto a crochet fabric. Just be careful to space out the crochet stitches evenly along the chosen edge.

Working a crochet edging directly onto a closely woven fabric takes a little more time, but it can be done. One method is to embroider a base of blanket stitches evenly along the edge and then crochet the edging onto this. Alternatively, use a fine crochet yarn and a sharp hook to pierce evenly spaced holes along the edge to work your stitches into.

Try working one of the simple edgings on pages 56–57 directly onto a dishtowel to see how easy it is. Use a small hook size with a point that will easily pierce the loosely woven fabric and a fine cotton crochet yarn.

Seams for crochet

There are various methods of joining two crocheted pieces together. You can do this either by crocheting them together, or by stitching them together with yarn and a blunt-ended yarn needle. Some seams are virtually invisible and can be used, for example, when joining together the back and front of a sweater. Others form a decorative feature in their own right and are used, for example, to join together several or many crocheted squares to make a pillow or throw. Use the swatches you have made for previous lessons to practice both stitched and crocheted seams. Good seams are essential for professional finishes.

Simple crocheted seams

Some crocheters swear by crocheted seams. They are quick to work and there is no need to thread a yarn needle to work them. You should definitely try them out and see if you might prefer to work your seams this way. They are useful for joining together crocheted squares for your first afghan!

Troubleshooting tips

- Before you join any crochet pieces together, block them into the correct shape and size (see page 15).

- For crocheted seams, use the same hook size you used for the crochet pieces.

- After completing a crocheted seam, open out the seam and press it lightly on the wrong side to flatten it.

Slip stitch seam

Using slip stitch produces a firm seam where minimal stretch in required. A different color of yarn is used here for the seam so that you can see the effect, but for an invisible seam you should use a matching yarn.

1 Place the pieces with right sides together, pinning if necessary. Join on the yarn with a slip knot as you would for starting a crochet edging (see page 52), but pull it through both layers close to the edge.

2 With the loop now at the front of the work, insert the hook through both layers again, a short distance to the right of the starting point as shown by the arrow. Wrap the yarn around the hook in the usual way and draw the yarn back through both layers and through the loop on the hook.

3 Working from right to left, continue working slip stitches in this way along the edge through both of the two pieces. Don't work the stitches too tightly. Work one slip stitch for every row end if you are working along the side edges, or for every stitch if you are working along the top or bottom edge of your crochet.

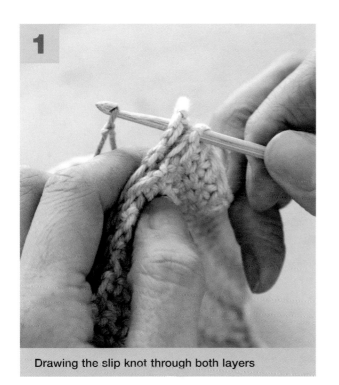

Drawing the slip knot through both layers

Inserting the hook to work the first slip stitch

Working repeating slip stitches along the seam

When finished and pressed, the slip stitch seam between the two pieces is flat and virtually invisible on the right side of the work.

Pulling the slip knot through the first pair of stitches

Working single crochet all along the seam

Single crochet seam

A single crochet seam is worked in the same way as a simple single crochet edging, but through two layers instead of one (see page 53). The single crochet seam shown here is being worked along two pieces of crochet that have each been edged with a row of single crochet. It creates a raised seam, which can be used as a decorative feature on the right side of the work if desired.

1 Place the pieces with right sides together (wrong sides together for a decorative seam). Insert the hook through the top of the first stitch on both layers and pull a slip knot through.

2 Make one chain (the turning chain for a single crochet stitch). Work the first single crochet into the same place as the slip knot. Work one single crochet through each pair of stitches all along the seam.

When the seam is worked on the right side of the crochet, it forms a decorative feature—more visible when worked in a contrasting color.

Crocheted zigzag seam

This zigzag seam is made of chain stitches and single crochet. It creates a highly decorative seam by zigzagging between the pieces of work. Use it for joining together afghan squares (see pages 96–101) or to make visible openwork seams on a summer garment, where it will enhance a delicate design. Alternatively, it would work well for joining crochet patches to fabric patches edged with blanket stitch.

Working the zigzag seam between crochet squares

If necessary, prepare the crochet squares you are joining together by working a single crochet edging around the outside edge (see page 53). Afghan squares, however, will not need another edging like this around them.

Lay two squares side by side, and join the yarn onto the corner stitch of one square (see page 52). Work one chain, one single crochet into the corresponding corner stitch of the other square, one chain, skip the next stitch on the first square and work one single crochet into the next stitch, one chain, one single crochet into the other square (again skipping a stitch). Work back and forth between the squares in this way to form the decorative zigzag seam.

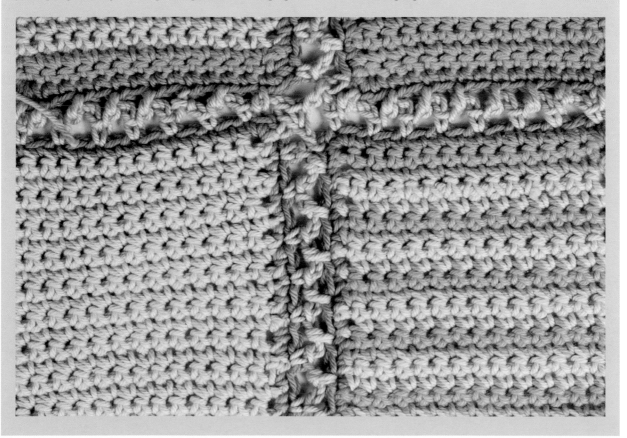

Stitched seams

There are several methods for stitching crochet together. The one you use will depend on your requirements. Before stitching the seams, block all crochet pieces (see page 15) and pin larger pieces together if necessary. Then thread matching yarn onto a large-eyed blunt-ended yarn needle.

If you are sewing a patchwork of squares together, arrange them on the floor before starting the seams.

Overcast seam

This is used mainly to join crocheted afghan squares. It is worked on the wrong side of the work.

1 Lay the pieces to be sewn together right side down on a flat surface. Secure the yarn to one edge, then insert the needle under two corresponding back loops on each edge and draw the yarn through.

2 Work in the same way all the way along the seam.

Mattress stitch

Use mattress stitch when you want an invisible seam. It is worked on the right side of the work.

1 Lay the pieces right side up on a flat surface. Secure the yarn to the lower edge of one piece, then make a short vertical stitch on the adjacent piece (under one or two rows).

2 Take a short vertical stitch on the other piece.

3 Work back and forth to each side in this way.

Making the first stitch on one piece

Backstitch seam

A backstitch seam is useful for joining pieces with uneven edges or if you want to alter a garment shape.

1 Place the pieces with the right sides together. Secure the yarn, then insert the needle from the front to the back to make a short stitch from right to left.

2 Insert the needle from back to front and bring it out at the center of the first stitch (a backward movement).

3 Continue working in this way along the seam.

Making the first forward stitch

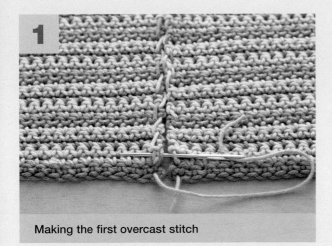

1 Making the first overcast stitch

2 Working overcast stitches up the seam

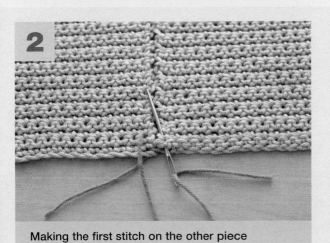

2 Making the first stitch on the other piece

3 Working in the same way up the seam

2 Making a backward stitch then a forward stitch

3 Working in the same way along the seam

project **three**

Patchwork pillow cover

The front of this pillow cover is made from four separate pieces of crochet. It is designed for you to practice your crocheted seams. The seams are worked in single crochet on the right side of the work as a design detail. Made in two pieces, the back of the cover forms an envelope opening so the pillow form can be taken out easily for washing.

Size
The finished pillow cover measures approximately 16in (40cm) by 16in (40cm).

What you need
Rowan *Denim* in three colors as follows:
A   Mid Denim (229)   6 x 1¾oz/50g balls
B   Indigo (225)   2 x 1¾oz/50g balls
C   Light Denim (231)   1 x 1¾oz/50g ball
Size G-6 (4mm) crochet hook
Two ¾–1in (2–2.5cm) buttons
Pillow form to fit finished cover

Troubleshooting tips

• The Rowan *Denim* yarn used here shrinks when washed, so you must wash the pieces and dry them as explained on the yarn label before sewing them together.

• If you want to test your gauge, crochet a swatch of single crochet, then wash and tumble dry the swatch before measuring across the stitches and rows (see page 14).

Gauge
After washing: 16 sts and 20 rows to 4in (10cm) measured over sc using size G-6 (4mm) hook *or size necessary to obtain correct gauge.*

Abbreviations
See page 13.

Front piece 1
Using size G-6 (4mm) hook and A, ch 42.
Row 1 (RS) 1 dc in 4th ch from hook, 1 dc in each of remaining ch, turn. *40 sts.*
Row 2 Ch 3 (counts as first st), skip first dc, *1 dc in next dc; rep from * to end, 1 dc in 3rd of 3-ch, turn.
Rows 3–21 [Rep row 2] 19 times.
Fasten off.

Front piece 2
Using size G-6 (4mm) hook and B, ch 31.
Row 1 (RS) 1 sc in 2nd ch from hook, 1 sc in each of remaining ch, turn. *30 sc.*
Row 2 Ch 1 (does NOT count as first st), 1 sc in each sc to end, turn.
Rows 3–29 [Rep row 2] 27 times. Fasten off.

Front piece 3
Using size G-6 (4mm) hook and B, ch 26.
Row 1 (RS) 1 sc in 2nd ch from hook, 1 sc in each of remaining ch, turn. *25 sc.*
Row 2 Ch 1 (does NOT count as first st), 1 sc in each sc to end, turn.
Rows 3–44 [Rep row 2] 42 times. Fasten off.

Front piece 4
Using size G-6 (4mm) hook and C, ch 32.
Row 1 (RS) 1 hdc in 3rd ch from hook, 1 hdc in each of remaining ch, turn. *30 hdc.*

Row 2 Ch 2 (does NOT count as first st), 1 hdc in each hdc to end, turn.
Rows 3–31 [Rep row 2] 29 times. Fasten off.

Back piece 1

Using size G-6 (4mm) hook and A, ch 65.
Row 1 (RS) 1 sc in 2nd ch from hook, 1 sc in each of remaining ch, turn. *64 sc.*
Row 2 Ch 1 (does NOT count as first st), 1 sc in each sc to end, turn.**
Rows 3–50 [Rep row 2] 48 times. Fasten off.

Back piece 2 (with buttonholes)

Work as for Back Piece 1 to **.
Rows 3–39 [Rep row 2] 37 times.
Row 40 Ch 1 (does NOT count as first st), 1 sc in each of first 21 sc, ch 2, skip 2 sc, 1 sc in each of next 18 sc, ch 2, skip 2 sc, 1 sc in each of last 21 sc, turn.
Row 41 Ch 1 (does NOT count as first st), 1 sc in each sc and 2 sc in each 2-ch space to end of row, turn.
Rows 42–46 [Rep row 2] 5 times. Fasten off.

Finishing

Wash all pieces at at 140°F (60°C) and tumble dry. Darn in yarn ends, then block all pieces (see page 15).

Troubleshooting tip

Remember that the single-crochet seams will be on the right side of the pillow cover. Take your time and crochet the stitches for the seams very carefully so they look neat and even. For the best results, practice the seam technique first on two crochet swatches following the instructions on page 62. When working the seam along row-end edges space the stitches evenly apart.

Pillow cover diagram

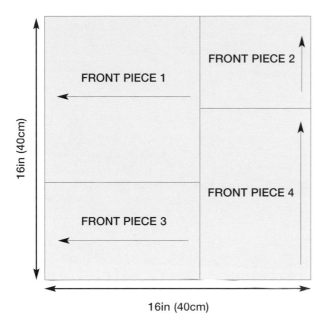

FRONT PIECE 1

FRONT PIECE 2

FRONT PIECE 3

FRONT PIECE 4

16in (40cm)

16in (40cm)

Crocheted seams

Place Front Pieces 2 and 4 together, with wrong side together and foundation-chain edge of Piece 2 aligned with top of last row of Piece 4 (the arrows on the diagram above indicate the direction of crocheting); then using size G-6 (4mm) hook and A, join together by working a row of sc through both layers. Fasten off. Using C, join together Front Pieces 1 and 3 in the same way, but with side edges of the pieces aligned. Using A, join together these two front panels in the same way (see diagram above).

Block prepared Front to 16in (40cm) square. Then pin two Back Pieces to Front, with wrong sides together and Back Piece with buttonholes overlapping on top of other Back Piece. Using size G-6 (4mm) hook and two strands of A together, and with Front facing, work a row of sc through both layers all around outer edge, working 3 sc into each corner, join with a sl st to first sc. Fasten off.

Sew on two buttons to correspond with buttonholes.

workshop
three

Basic crochet shaping

In this workshop, we look at simple ways to create different shapes of crochet, both for rectangular crochet pieces and those worked in circles (known as "in the round").

Basic increasing and decreasing

Basic increasing and decreasing is worked by varying the numbers of stitches in the rows so that your crochet is no longer straight-sided, but slopes at an angle. The angle of the slope will be determined by the numbers of stitches increased or decreased, and by the frequency (every row or every other row for example). On flat crochet you usually increase and decrease at the side edges, but you can increase or decrease in the center of the work to create attractive shaping lines. More sophisticated forms of shaping are shown in Workshop Five for basic garments.

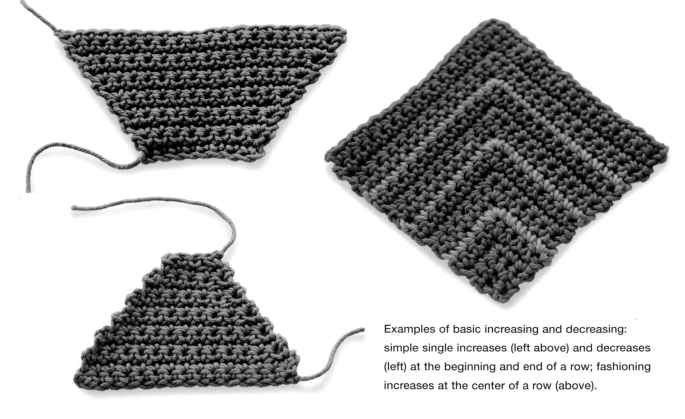

Examples of basic increasing and decreasing: simple single increases (left above) and decreases (left) at the beginning and end of a row; fashioning increases at the center of a row (above).

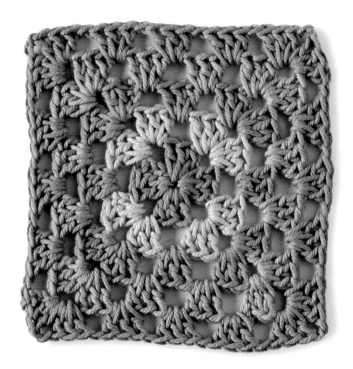

Examples of shapes worked in the round, from the center outward: a simple single crochet afghan square (top left); a traditional double crochet afghan square (above); and a simple three-round flower shape (left).

Crochet in the round

In addition to working crochet in rectangles, you can work it in rounds. This is a useful technique for making tubular or cylindrical objects, something you cannot do as successfully in knitting. You can work a hat or a circular bag without a seam, for example. The most well-known example of this form of crochet is the afghan square or crochet motif—hugely popular for making patchwork throws and pillows, often from scraps of leftover yarns.

The shaping patterns shown in this chapter are all worked in basic stitches, but you can, of course, vary the stitch pattern—the techniques remain the same in principle.

1

Working two stitches into the first stitch

2

Working two stitches into the last stitch

Simple increases

The simplest form of increasing for shape is done by working two stitches into the first and last stitches of the previous row. (Other forms of increasing, such as working more than two stitches into an existing stitch, are discussed on page 143.) Make a swatch of single crochet to try out this simple increasing technique and the decreases on the following page.

Increasing a stitch at side edges

1 At the beginning of the row, work a turning chain of the required length (here, one chain, as you are working in single crochet). Then work one stitch into the first stitch of the previous row in the usual way. Next, work another stitch into the first stitch to create the increase.

2 Continue to the last stitch of the row. Work a stitch into the last stitch in the usual way, then work one more stitch into the last stitch to make the increase.

For details of how to work more complex increases, see pages 143–145.

Here, increases have been worked in single crochet at each end of every alternate row to produce a smooth, gradual increase on both sides of the piece.

Simple decreases

The simplest form of decreasing is done by simply skipping a stitch in the previous row. This form of decreasing is usually used in single crochet because the stitches are short, and if you skip a stitch it hardly shows. For taller stitches, other methods apply (see pages 140–141).

Decreasing a stitch at side edges

1 At the beginning of the row, work a turning chain of the required length (here, one chain, as you are working in single crochet). Then to decrease one stitch, skip the first stitch of the previous row and work your first stitch into the second stitch.

2 Work up to the last two stitches at the end of the row. To decrease one stitch, skip the next stitch and work into the last stitch of the row.

Here, decreases have been worked in single crochet at each end of every alternate row to produce edges that slant inward.

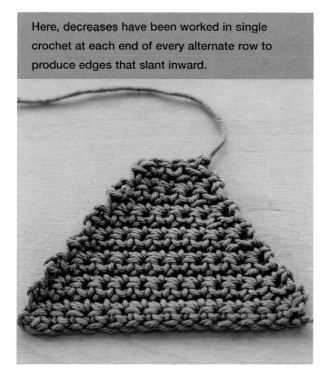

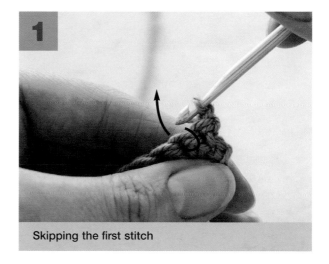

Skipping the first stitch

Skipping the second to last stitch

For details of how to work more complex decreases, see pages 138–142.

Fashioning increases and decreases

Increasing and decreasing in the middle of the row creates a noticeable textured mark on the fabric if the increase or decrease is worked at the same point in the fabric. This is known as a "fashioning mark," and some patterns use this as a way of creating a "dart" in the front and back panels of garments. Working increases or decreases in the center of a row, rather than the edges, also creates a smoother line at the edge of the fabric, which is useful if the seams will be visible.

Working a mid-row increase

1 Work to the center of the row, and then work two single crochet (or required number of stitches) into the same stitch of the row below.

2 For a gradual increase that creates a gentle bend in the fabric, work two single crochet (or the required number of stitches) at the same position on every alternate row.

Working two single crochet into the same stitch

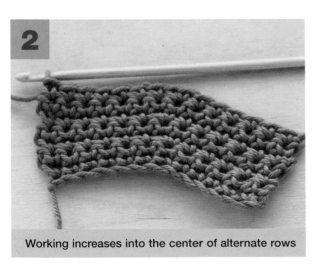

Working increases into the center of alternate rows

Working an increase into the center of every row gives a more pronounced effect.

Working a mid-row decrease

1 Work to the center of the row. Skip one stitch and insert the hook into the next stitch (as shown by the arrow).

2 Complete the stitch in the usual way. For a gradual decrease, continue to work a decrease in this way at the same position in the middle of every alternate row. For a more pronounced effect, decrease on every row.

Skipping a stitch to create the decrease

Working into the next stitch after the skipped stitch

Here, decreases have been worked into the center of alternate rows, which gives a gradual, curving shape.

Troubleshooting tips

• If increases are made at the same point on the work and repeated over a few rows, the increase or shaping line can move to the right or to the left. Use a marker to indicate where the increase position is. If you would like to shape to the right, work the increase in the stitch before the marker; to shape to the left, work the increase in the stitch after the marker.

• Working 3 sc into one stitch creates a corner effect. This method is used in afghan squares to produce a regular square shape (see page 93).

• Working 2 sc into the same stitch gives a more gradual increase. This kind of increase is often used in circles.

Working in the round

The techniques shown here for making a simple crochet circle are used to create not only flat circles, but flowers, bowls, bags, geometric shapes, and squares. Crochet in the round is usually worked with the right side always facing toward you, and in most patterns each round is joined into a complete circle with a slip stitch connecting the first and last stitches. Learn how to make a simple crochet circle, before trying out some crochet flower and afghan motifs.

Starting a circle

A crochet circle is usually started with a foundation of a simple ring of chain stitches. Make your first circle using this method, then try out the ring variations on pages 82–83.

Making a simple foundation ring

1 Make six chain (your pattern will always tell you how many chains to work—usually about one chain for every two stitches in the first round). Then begin a slip stitch by inserting the hook into the first chain made.

2 Wrap the yarn around the hook and draw it through both the chain and the loop on the hook to complete the slip stitch and form the ring.

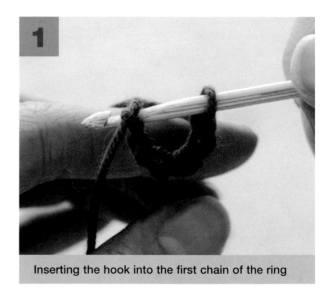

Inserting the hook into the first chain of the ring

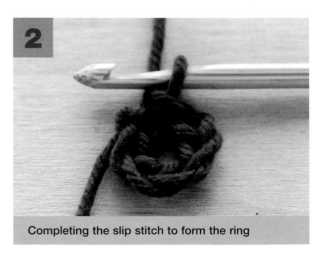

Completing the slip stitch to form the ring

Working into a chain space

A *chain space* is a space under one or more chain stitches in crochet fabric. When a pattern tells you to work stitches "into the chain space," insert your hook *under* the chain and *through* the space. This method is also used for working the first round of stitches into the foundation ring of a circle.

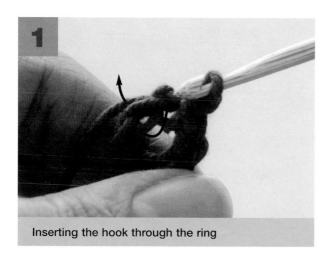

Inserting the hook through the ring

Working stitches into the ring

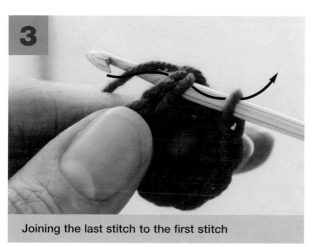

Joining the last stitch to the first stitch

Working the first round of a circle

Before you start the first round, you need to work a turning chain just as when working rows even though you do not turn the work (see page 29). The turning chain sometimes counts as the first stitch of the round but not always. For example, with single crochet (used for this sample), the turning chain does NOT count as the first stitch, but for the taller stitches it does.

1 Work a one-chain turning chain so that the work is at the right level to start the round of single crochet. Then insert the hook through the center of the foundation ring as shown by the arrow, to begin the first stitch.

2 Begin to work ten single crochet into the ring, pushing the stitches closer together if necessary to fit them all into the ring and catching the yarn end inside the stitches so there is no need to darn it in later.

3 After working all ten stitches, join the last stitch to the first by working a slip stitch through the top of the first single crochet of the round.

The first round of the circle completed. You are now ready to crochet the second round.

Working two stitches into the same stitch

Working two stitches into each stitch

The second round completed. A slip stitch is used at the end of each round to join the last stitch of the round to the first stitch of the same round.

Working the second round of a circle

The second round, as the first, begins with a turning chain. Remember that the turning chain itself does NOT count as a the first stitch of a round for single crochet (your crochet pattern will always tell you whether the first stitch counts as a stitch or not). On the second round, you need to start increasing the number of stitches in order to keep the circle flat.

1 Work one turning chain so that you are ready to start the second round of single crochet stitches. Then work the first single crochet into the same stitch that you worked the slip stitch into at the end of the previous round. (The stitch the slip stitch is worked into at the end of the previous round is always the base for the first stitch of a round.) Then work one more single crochet into the same place as the first single crochet to increase one stitch. Work two single crochet into the next stitch as shown.

2 Continue working two stitches into each single crochet of the previous round as shown. At the end of the round join the last stitch to the first by working a slip stitch into the top of the first single crochet.

Working a flat circle

After working just two rounds following the step-by-step instructions on the previous pages, you will have understood the basics of creating a flat circle of crochet: as the rounds of stitches progress outward from the center, you keep increasing stitches around the circle to keep it flat. Your pattern will tell you how many stitches to increase in a round. (If you stop increasing, the crochet will grow upward in a tube shape.) Work this simple striped circle to try out your new skills.

To join in a new color at the beginning of a round use the same technique as for joining in a new color when working an edging (see page 52).

Striped circle

Striped circle

This motif is worked using four colors: A, B, C, and D. Using A, ch 6 and join with a sl st to first ch to form a ring.

Round 1 (RS) Ch 3 (to count as first dc), 11 dc in ring, join with a sl st to 3rd of 3-ch at beg of round. *12 sts.* Fasten off A.

Round 2 (RS) Join B to any dc, ch 1 (does NOT count as first st), 2 sc in same dc as 1-ch, *2 sc in next dc; rep from * to end, join with a sl st to first sc. *24 sc.* Fasten off B.

Round 3 (WS) With WS facing, join A to any sc, ch 1 (does NOT count as first st), 1 sc in same place as 1-ch, 1 sc in next sc, 2 sc in next sc, *1 sc in each of next 2 sc, 2 sc in next sc; rep from * to end, join with a sl st to first sc. *32 sc.* Fasten off A.

Round 4 (RS) With RS facing, join C to any sc, ch 3 (counts as first dc), 1 dc in each of next 2 sc, 2 dc in next sc, *1 dc in each of next 3 sc, 2 dc in next sc; rep from * to end, join with a sl st to 3rd of 3-ch at beg of round. *40 sts.* Fasten off C.

Round 5 (RS) With RS facing, join D to back loop of any dc, ch 1 (does NOT count as first st), working into only back loop of top of each st, work 1 sc in same dc as 1-ch, *1 sc in next dc; rep from * to end, join with a sl st to first sc. Fasten off D.

Small hole variation

To create a smaller hole at the center of a circle (see below), you can work all the stitches of the first round into a single chain.

To do this for a first round of single crochet, make two chains, then work the required number of stitches into the second chain from the hook. At the  end of the round, join the last stitch to the first by working a slip stitch into the top of the first single crochet.

Foundation ring variations

Here are two other methods for making foundation rings to add to your repertoire. Both methods can be used to form open or closed holes at the center of the ring.

Drawstring ring

Sometimes—if you are working a hat or a bag, for example—it's important to create a shape without a hole at the center. With this ring method you can very easily tighten the hole to completely close the center. It is also convenient because you can work the first round of stitches easily into an open ring and tighten it into a circle of the desired tightness afterward.

1 Form a ring with the yarn, with the tail end of the yarn on top. Insert the hook through the center of this ring and draw a loop through it.

2 Work one chain and then work the required number of single crochet into the ring, catching in the yarn tail.

3 Pull the yarn end as shown, to close the drawstring ring. Then complete the round by working a slip stitch into the first single crochet of the round.

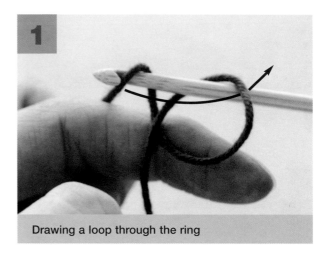

Drawing a loop through the ring

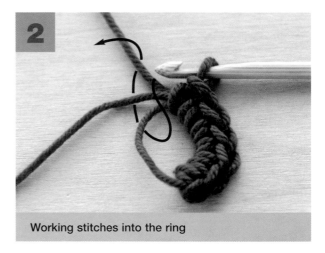

Working stitches into the ring

Finished closed drawstring ring

Pulling the yarn end to close the ring

Padded ring

The padded foundation ring forms a more obvious, slightly three-dimensional ring at the center of the shape. It is often used for flowers and is common in Irish crochet lace motifs.

1 Wrap the yarn six to ten times around one finger (depending on the thickness of the yarn you are using). Here the ring is being wrapped around the index finger, but you can use your little finger for a smaller hole.

2 Slip the wrapped ring off your finger, holding it carefully to maintain the circular shape. Then insert the hook through the center of the ring and draw a loop of yarn through the ring. Work one chain, and then work the required number of single crochet stitches for the first round. At the end of the round join the last stitch with the first by working a a slip stitch into the first single crochet in the usual way to complete the round. To tighten the hole, if desired, pull the yarn end and darn it into the padded ring to secure it.

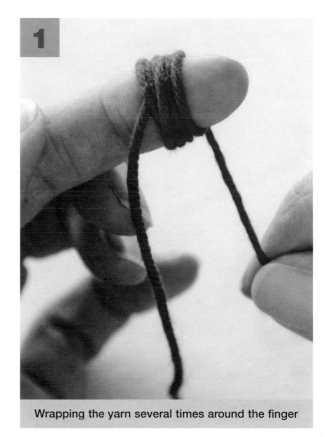

Wrapping the yarn several times around the finger

Finished padded ring

Working the first round into the padded ring

Crochet flowers

Little crochet flowers make great embellishments for bags, hats, pillow covers, and other crochet projects. You begin most crochet flowers by working the first round into a foundation ring or into a single chain. Working in rounds with just a few simple stitches, you can then create a wide range of different effects. Here is one flower pattern shown step by step to help you learn the basics. Alternative flower designs are given on pages 86–89.

Working a two-color flower

This flower has a very small hole at the center, which is created by working the first round of stitches into a single chain (see Small Hole Variation on page 81). It is made using two colors—A and B.

1 Using color A, ch 2, work 7 sc in second ch from hook, then join with a sl st to first sc to complete first round. Next, ch 3 to begin second round.

2 For second round, then *work [1 dc, ch 3, 1 dc] all in next sc; repeat from * five times, 1 dc in same place as sl st of previous round (at base of 3-ch at beginning of round), ch 3.

3 To complete second round, join with a sl st to top of 3-ch at beginning of round—*seven 3-ch spaces have been made*. Fasten off A.

4 To begin third round, join B (see page 95) to any 3-ch space of previous round, ch 1, 7 sc in same 3-ch space.

5 To complete third round, skip next dc, 1 sl st in next dc, *7 sc in next 3-ch space, skip next dc, 1 sl st in next dc; repeat from * to end of round, join with a sl st to first sc of round. Fasten off B.

Beginning the second round with three chains

Beginning the third round with a contrasting color

2

Working the second round

3

The second round completed

5

Working the petals of the third round

The completed flower.

Clematis

Rose

Anemone

Primula

Two-color daisy

Crochet flower patterns

Here is a selection of crochet flower designs for you to try out, including the pattern for the simple two-color flower on pages 84–85 (called Primula below). You could use them to make simple brooches to pin to hats, bags, or coats. Choose any yarn you like for your flower brooch and sew a safety pin to the back.

When joining in a new color on the flowers, use one of the methods on pages 94–95.

Primula

This simple bicolor flower is completed in just three simple rounds and is worked in single crochet and double crochet.

What you need

Rowan *4-ply Cotton* or *Cotton Glace* in 2 colors: **A** and **B**
Size C-2 (2.5mm) crochet hook

To make flower

Using size C-2 (2.5mm) hook and A, ch 2.
Round 1 7 sc in 2nd ch from hook, join with a sl st to first sc.
Round 2 Ch 3, *work [1 dc, ch 3, 1 dc] all in next sc; rep from * 5 times, 1 dc in same place as sl st at end of previous round, ch 3, join with a sl st to 3rd of 3-ch at beg of round. *7 3-ch spaces made.* Fasten off A.
Round 3 Join B to any 3-ch space, ch 1, 7 sc in same 3-ch space, skip next dc, 1 sl st in next dc, *7 sc in next 3-ch space, skip next dc, 1 sl st in next dc; rep from * to end of round, join with a sl st to first sc. Fasten off B.

Clematis

The petals on this flower are made individually and sewn together, so you can adjust the pattern to have as many or as few petals as you like. Each petal is worked by using both sides of the foundation chain, which gives it a central spine or vein. It could also be used as a leaf pattern. For a different look, use a small vintage button for the center instead of the spot.

What you need

Rowan *4-ply Cotton* or *Cotton Glace* in 3 colors: **A**, **B**, and **C**
Size C-2 (2.5mm) crochet hook

Petals (make 5)

Using size C-2 (2.5mm) hook and A, ch 8.
Row 1 1 sc in 2nd ch from hook, 1 hdc in next ch, 1 dc in each of next 2 ch, 3 dc in next ch, 1 hdc in next ch, 1 sc in last ch, continuing along other side of foundation ch, work 1 sc in same ch as last sc, 1 hdc in next ch, 3 dc in next ch, 1 dc in each of next 2 ch, 1 hdc in next ch, 1 sc in last ch. Fasten off.
Using photograph as a guide, arrange the petals in a flower shape, overlapping slightly at the center, and sew them together.

Center flower

Using size C-2 (2.5mm) hook and B, ch 2.
Round 1 8 sc in 2nd ch from hook, join with a sl st to first sc.
Round 2 *Ch 3, work [1 dc, ch 3, 1 sl st] all in same place as last sl st, 1 sl st in next sc; rep from * to end of round. Fasten off.

Center spot

Using size C-2 (2.5mm) hook and C, make a drawstring ring and work 5 sc in ring (see page 82), pull ring closed and join with a sl st to first sc. Fasten off.

Assembling the flower

Sew three pieces together as shown.

Anemone

Crochet has a natural tendency to curl when worked in narrow strips, and this is exploited to create the central stamens on this flower.

What you need

Rowan *4-ply Cotton* or *Cotton Glace* in 2 colors: **A** and **B**

Size C-2 (2.5mm) crochet hook

To make flower

Using size C-2 (2.5mm) hook and B, ch 4 and join with an sl st to first ch to form a ring.

Round 1 Ch 1 (does NOT count as first st), 12 sc in ring, join with a sl st to first sc.

Round 2 *Ch 6, 1 sc in 2nd ch from hook, 1 sc in each of rem 4 ch, 1 sl st in same sc as last sl st, [turn, ch 1, 1 sc in each of 5 sc of petal] twice, 1 sl st in each of next 2 sc of round 1 to complete petal; rep from * 5 times. *6 petals made.*

Round 3 *1 sc in each of next 5 ch up side of petal, 5 sc in space between last sc worked into and next sc, 1 sc in each of next 5 sc down other side of petal, 1 sl st in a sl st between petals; rep from * to end of round. Fasten off.

Stamens (make 4)

Using size C-2 (2.5mm) hook and A, ch 6.

Row 1 1 sc in 2nd ch from hook, 1 sc in each of rem 4 ch. Fasten off.

Use yarn ends to fasten stamens around center circle as shown.

Two-color daisy

This is a delicate flower formed by working the second round of stitches into the front loop of the stitches of the first round, and the stitches of the third round into the back loops of the stitches of the first round. This produces a two-color flower without the hassle of having to stitch two pieces together!

You will need

Rowan *4-ply Cotton* or *Cotton Glace* in 2 colors: **A** and **B**

Size D-3 (3mm) crochet hook

To make flower

Using size D-3 (3mm) and A, ch 4 and join with a sl st to first ch to form a ring.

Round 1 Ch 1 (does NOT count as a first st), 12 sc in ring, join with a sl st to first sc.

Round 2 Working sts into front loops only of sc of previous round, work *ch 4, 1 sl st in same place as last sl st, 1 sl st in next sc; rep from * 11 times. *12 4-ch loops made.* Fasten off A.

Round 3 With RS facing and working sts into back loops only of sc of round 1, join B to any sc of round 1, ch 3, work [1 dc, ch 3, 1 sl st] all in same place B was joined, 1 sl st in next sc, *ch 3, work [1 dc, ch 3, 1 sl st] all in same place as last sl st, 1 sl st in next sc; rep from * 10 times. Fasten off B.

Rose with button center

This flower is made up of a larger outer flower with six petals and a small separate center. It is topped with a button covered with a piece of knitting. Knitting the cover is optional. If you prefer, cover the button with fabric or use a plain button in a suitable color. (See the box on the next page for more ideas for the button center.)

What you need

Rowan *Handknit Cotton* in 3 colors: **A**, **B**, and **C**

Size G-6 (4mm) crochet hook

Size 4 (3.5mm) knitting needles

Metal button to cover, ¾in (2cm) in diameter (optional)
Blunt-ended yarn needle

Flower center

Using size G-6 (4mm) hook and A, ch 8 and join with
a sl st in first ch to form a ring.
Round 1 Ch 1, 16 sc in ring, join with a sl st to first sc.
Round 2 Ch 1 (does NOT count as first st), 1 sc in
same place as sl st, ch 5, *skip 1 sc, 1 sc in next sc,
ch 5; rep from * to end of round, join with a sl st to
first sc. Fasten off.

Outer flower

Using size G-6 (4mm) hook and A, ch 8 and join with
a sl st in first ch to form a ring.
Round 1 Ch 6, *1 dc in ring, ch 3; rep from * 4 times,
join with a sl st to 3rd of 6-ch at beg of round.
Round 2 Ch 1, work [1 sc, 1 hdc, 3 dc, 1 hdc, 1 sc]
all in next 3-ch space; rep from * to end of round.
6 petals made.
Round 3 *Ch 5, inserting hook from back work 1 sc in
next dc of *round 1*; rep from * to end of round, ending
with ch 5.
Round 4 *Work [1 sc, 1 hdc, 5 dc, 1 hdc, 1 sc] all in
next 5-ch space; rep from * to end of round.
Round 5 *Ch 7, inserting hook from back work 1 sc in
next sc of *round 3*; rep from * to end of round, ending
with ch 7.
Round 6 *Work [1 sc, 1 hdc, 7 dc, 1 hdc, 1 sc] all in
next 7-ch space; rep from * to end of round, join with
a sl st to first sc. Fasten off.

Knitted covered button (optional)

Using size 4 (3.5mm) knitting needles and C, cast on
7 sts and work 10 rows in stockinette stitch.
Cut off yarn leaving a tail end 4in (10cm) long. Thread
end onto a blunt-ended yarn needle, pass needle
through stitches and pull to gather knitted fabric.
Place curved side of button on the right side of knitted

fabric and sew diagonally from side to side, gathering
the fabric and pulling it taut over the button. Secure
yarn firmly and leave end to sew button in place.

Assembling the flower

Place Flower Center on top of Outer Flower, with
button on top, and sew all three pieces together.

Alternatives for button center on Rose flower motif

- You can cover any size of button, but bigger
  buttons are easier to work with.

- Seed stitch would also be an effective stitch to
  use as an alternative to stockinette stitch for
  the button covering.

- When covering the button, make sure you
  don't pull the knitted fabric too tight or you will
  see the button color through it. If your button
  color is still showing through, try using a
  smaller size knitting needle to create a denser
  fabric.

- If you cannot knit, you can cover the button for
  the center of the flower with a suitable fabric
  instead. Before stretching the fabric over the
  button, embroider it with a small chain-stitch
  flower worked in a contrasting yarn.

- As an alternative to a covered button, choose
  a button with four holes and sew it on with a
  contrasting yarn, working a cross through
  the holes.

project **four**

Cloche hat with flower

Made in simple single crochet with a double crochet edging, this hat shows how sculptured shapes can be made in the round. Use the Anemone flower on page 88 for the hat trim as here, or choose one of the other flowers on pages 86–89.

To reduce or increase the circumference of the hat, simply add or delete one increase round for every 1¼in (3cm) you want to reduce or enlarge the hat.

Size
To fit head circumference 21¾–23½in (54–60cm)

What you need
Two 1¾oz/50g balls of Rowan *RYC Cashsoft DK* in **A** (Bloom 520)
One ⅞oz/25g ball of Rowan *Kidsilk Haze* in **B** (Liqueur 595)
Size G-6 (4mm) crochet hook
Blunt-ended yarn needle
Safety pin (if the corsage is to be removable)

Gauge
16 sts and 24 rows to 4in (10cm) measured over sc using size G-6 (4mm) hook *or size necessary to obtain correct gauge.*

Abbreviations
See page 13.

Hat
Using A, make a drawstring ring (see page 82), then using size G-6 (4mm) hook, beg as follows:
Round 1 (RS) Draw a loop through center of ring, ch 1 (does NOT count as first st), 10 sc in ring, pull end of yarn to close ring, join with a sl st to first sc. (Do not turn at end of rounds, but work with RS always facing.)

Round 2 Ch 1 (does NOT count as first st), 1 sc in same place as sl st, 2 sc in next sc, *1 sc in next sc, 2 sc in next sc; rep from * 3 times, join with a sl st to first sc. *15 sc.*

Round 3 Ch 1, 1 sc in same place as sl st, 1 sc in next sc, 2 sc in next sc, *1 sc in each of next 2 sc, 2 sc in next sc; rep from * 3 times, join with a sl st to first sc. *20 sc.*

Round 4 Ch 1, 1 sc in same place as sl st, 1 sc in each of next 2 sc, 2 sc in next sc, *1 sc in each of next 3 sc, 2 sc in next sc; rep from * 3 times, join with a sl st to first sc. *25 sc.*

Work 6 rounds more in this way, working one more sc between increases on each round. *35 sc.*

Round 11 Ch 1, 1 sc in same place as sl st, 1 sc in each of next 9 sc, 2 sc in next sc, *1 sc in each of next 10 sc, 2 sc in next sc; rep from * 3 times, join with a sl st to first sc. *60 sc.*

Round 12 Ch 1, 1 sc in same place as sl st, 1 sc in each sc to end of round, join with a sl st to first sc.

Round 13 Ch 1, 1 sc in same place as sl st, 1 sc in each of next 10 sc, 2 sc in next sc, *1 sc in each of next 11 sc, 2 sc in next sc; rep from * 3 times, join with a sl st to first sc. *65 sc.*

Round 14 Rep round 12.

Round 15 Ch 1, 1 sc in same place as sl st, 1 sc in each of next 11 sc, 2 sc in next sc, *1 sc in each of next 12 sc, 2 sc in next sc; rep from * 3 times, join with a sl st to first sc. *70 sc.*

Round 16 Rep round 12.

Round 17 Ch 1, 1 sc in same place as sl st, 1 sc in each of next 12 sc, 2 sc in next sc, *1 sc in each of next 13 sc, 2 sc in next sc; rep from * 3 times, join with a sl st to first sc. *75 sts.*

Round 18 Rep round 12.

Round 19 Ch 1, 1 sc in same place as sl st, 1 sc in

each of next 13 sc, 2 sc in next sc, *1 sc in each of next 14 sc, 2 sc in next sc; rep from * 3 times, join with a sl st to first sc. *80 sc.*

Round 20 Rep round 12.

Round 21 Ch 1, 1 sc in same place as sl st, 1 sc in each of next 14 sc, 2 sc in next sc, *1 sc in each of next 15 sc, 2 sc in next sc; rep from * 3 times, join with a sl st to first sc. *85 sc.*

Rounds 22–49 [Rep round 12] 28 times. Fasten off. Pull yarn end at Hat center and secure firmly on WS.

Flower

Work as for the Anemone on page 88, but using size G-6 (4mm) hook and 2 strands of B held together for petals and one strand of A for stamens.

Hat edging

Using 2 strands of B held together and with RS of Hat facing, join yarn to any sc in last round of Hat, *skip 1 sc, 5 dc in next sc, skip 1 sc, 1 sl st in next sc; rep from * to end of round, join with a sl st to same place yarn was joined in.

Darn in any yarn ends.

Fold back a 2in (5cm) brim and press lightly.

Sew flower to hat, or sew flower to safety pin and attach to brim, using flower to hold brim in place.

Method 1—Working the first corner

Making an afghan square

Afghan squares (also known as granny squares) evolved as a method of using up scraps of yarn, and come in all shapes and sizes, from squares and circles to hexagons and octagons. They are worked in the round, and can be made into blankets or throws (also known as afghans), shawls, bags, pillow covers—the list goes on.

As you make the same shape over and over, they're also an easy and portable project. There is a myriad of different patterns, allowing you to mix and match designs, shapes, and even sizes. Simply varying the colors on the same shape will produce a really different look. You can add an extra touch of individuality and decoration to your design when you assemble the squares—for example, by working single crochet seams on the right side of the work in a contrasting color (see page 62).

Method 1—Working the third corner

Method 1—the completed single crochet square. Make the square as big as you like, working all rounds in the same way as the second round.

Increasing in rounds on a geometric shape

Afghan squares begin with a foundation ring—just like the flowers on pages 86–89. Increasing at the same four positions on each round creates the angled corners. To illustrate the technique used for forming corners, here are two common methods, one for single crochet and one for double crochet.

Method 1

This is the basic method for making a simple single crochet square. The corners are created by working three stitches into the corners on every round.

1 Ch 4 and join with a sl st to first ch to form a ring. For the first round, ch 1, 8 sc in ring and fasten off the first color. For the second round, join the new color to any sc (see page 94), ch 1, 3 sc in same place as new color was joined in to form the first corner.

2 Then work 1 sc in next sc, *3 sc in next sc, 1 sc in next sc; repeat from * twice, join with a sl st to first sc. On the following rounds, work 3 sc in the center sc of each 3-sc group at each corner and 1 sc in all other sc.

Method 2

This is a method often used for double crochet. Groups of double crochet with a chain space at the center are worked into each corner, and on subsequent rows the corner stitches are worked into the corner chain spaces of the previous round. This creates small holes at the corners. The same method can be used to create any geometric shape, such as a hexagon or octagon, simply by varying the number of groups of stitches and chain spaces to create the corners.

Ch 6 and join with a sl st to first ch to form a ring. For the first round, ch 3, 2 dc in ring, ch 1 (to form first corner), *3 dc in ring, ch 1; repeat from * twice, join with a sl st to 3rd of first 3-ch and fasten off the first color.

On every following round, work 1 dc in each dc and and work [2 dc, ch 1, 2 dc] all in each corner.

Method 2—Working a corner in the first round

Method 2—two rounds completed on the double crochet square. To work more rounds, follow the Simple Striped Square pattern on pages 98–99.

Perfecting your afghan motifs

- **Working a motif with only two colors:** If you are working a motif in only two colors, fasten off the old yarn and join in the new color rather than keeping both yarns attached. This avoids yarn tangles and untidy stranding on the back of the work.

- **Alternative method for joining in a new yarn:** Some patterns will tell you to join in a new "with a slip stitch." To do this, simply insert the hook through the specified stitch or space and draw a loop through this stitch or space. Then work the next stitch (usually a chain) in the usual way. This method is a common one, but does not produce as secure an attachment as the two methods shown right.

- **Where to join on the yarn on your motif:** Your pattern will always tell you where to join on a new yarn. Follow this instruction carefully to ensure that you work the remainder of the round into the correct stitches.

- **Slip stitch that joins the end of a round to the beginning:** It is easy to confuse this slip stitch with the other stitches of the previous round. Remember to ignore this stitch at the end of the following round and do not work into it.

- **To fasten off after a slip stitch:** When you "fasten off" after a slip stitch, cut the yarn and draw the end through the center of the slip stitch. If you are starting a new round after fastening off, work over the yarn end so you don't have to darn in the end later.

Joining in new colors on motifs

You can create lovely and varied effects on your afghan motifs by using different colors of yarn for different rounds. Changing colors is much easier than you may think! Here are two handy techniques for joining in a new color at the beginning of a round.

Tie-in method

With this method, the new yarn is simply tied to a space.

Tie a simple knot through the space where the next round is to begin, leaving a tail about 2¾in (7cm) long. Insert the hook through the space where the knot has been made, wrap the yarn around the hook using the ball end of the yarn and draw a loop through. Then work the round following your pattern. You can either work over the yarn end or darn it in afterward.

Tied in yarn, ready to use on the next round.

Pulling the slip knot through the motif

Making the first chain stitch

Slip-knot method

This method uses a slip knot (the first thing you learn to make in crochet) to join in the new color. It is the same technique used for joining in a new yarn when working an edging onto a finished piece of crochet (see page 52), only here you are working in the round, and sometimes joining the yarn into a chain space rather than a stitch.

1 Make a slip knot and place it behind the afghan motif. Insert the hook from front to back through the motif (either through a space or a stitch) and pull the loop through to the front of the work.

2 Continue the round following your crochet pattern. Once you have worked the first chain of the round, the slip knot will be firmly secured to the motif. Either work over the yarn end or darn it in afterward.

The new yarn is now joined in and you can continue with your pattern.

Afghan motif patterns

Here is a selection of afghan square patterns that can be turned into throws, scarves, or pillow covers in whatever colors you like. Try working the Traditional Afghan square first because it is very easy to memorize the pattern once you have made one or two. Remember that afghan squares are worked in rounds with the right side of the work always facing you *unless* the pattern states otherwise.

Traditional afghan square

Afghan star

Small flower squares

Traditional afghan square

This square is worked using five colors: A, B, C, D, and E.

Note: For a smaller square, work just the first three or four rounds.

Using A, make a drawstring ring (see page 82) and begin rounds as follows:

Round 1 Insert hook through ring, yo and draw a loop through ring, ch 3, 2 dc in ring, ch 3, [3 dc in ring, ch 3] 3 times, pull yarn tail to close ring and join with a sl st to 3rd of 3-ch at beg of round. Fasten off A.

Round 2 Join B to any 3-ch space, ch 3, work [2 dc, ch 3, 3 dc] all in same space, ch 1, work *[3 dc, ch 3, 3 dc] all in next 3-ch space, ch 1; rep from * twice, join with a sl st to 3rd of 3-ch at beg of round. Fasten off B.

Round 3 Join C to any 3-ch space (a corner space), ch 3, [2 dc, ch 3, 3 dc] all in same space, ch 1, *3 dc in next 1-ch space, ch 1, work [3 dc, ch 3, 3 dc] all in next 3-ch space, ch 1; rep from * twice, 3 dc in next 1-ch space, ch 1, join with a sl st to 3rd of 3-ch at beg of round. Fasten off C.

Round 4 Join D to any 3-ch space (a corner space), ch 3, [2 dc, ch 3, 3 dc] all in same space, *[ch 1, 3 dc in next 1-ch space] twice, ch 1, work [3 dc, ch 3, 3 dc] all in next 3-ch space; rep from * twice, [ch 1, 3 dc in next 1-ch space] twice, ch 1, join with a sl st to 3rd of 3-ch at beg of round. Fasten off D.

Round 4 Join E to any 3-ch space (a corner space), ch 3, [2 dc, ch 3, 3 dc] all in same space, *[ch 1, 3 dc in next 1-ch space] 3 times, ch 1, work [3 dc, ch 3, 3 dc] all in next 3-ch space; rep from * twice, [ch 1, 3 dc in next 1-ch space] 3 times, ch 1, join with a sl st to 3rd of 3-ch at beg of round. Fasten off E.

Afghan star

This square is worked using two colors: A and B. Using A, ch 6 and join with a sl st to first ch to form a ring.

Round 1 (RS) Ch 1, 12 sc in ring, join with a sl st to first sc. (Do not turn at the end of the rounds until the pattern tells you to.)

Round 2 Ch 3, work 1 dc same place as last sl st, *2 dc next sc; rep from * to end of round, join with a sl st to 3rd of 3-ch at beg of round. *24 sts.* Fasten off A.

Round 3 Join B to same place as last sl st, ch 4, 1 tr in same place as B was joined in, 1 tr in next dc, *2 tr in next dc, 1 tr in next dc; rep from * to end of round, join with a sl st to 4th of 4-ch at beg of round. *36 sts.* Fasten off B.

Round 4 Join A to same place as last sl st, ch 3, 2 dc in *space* before first tr of previous row, [skip next 3 tr from previous row and work 3 dc in *space* before next tr (between the stitches)] twice, *skip next 3 tr, then work corner by working [3 dc, ch 1, 3 dc] all in space before next tr, [skip next 3 tr from previous row and work 3 dc in *space* before next tr] twice; rep from *twice, 3 dc in same place as first 3-ch and 2 dc were worked, ch 1, join with a sl st to 3rd of 3-ch at beg of round, then turn (so WS is facing for next round).

Round 5 (WS) Work 1 sl st in first 1-ch, ch 3, 2 dc in same space as last sl st, *[3 dc in space between next two 3-dc groups] 3 times, work [3 dc, ch 1, 3 dc] all in corner 1-ch space; rep from * twice, [3 dc in space between next two 3-dc groups] 3 times, 3 dc in same place as first 3-ch and 2 dc were worked, ch 1, join with a sl st to 3rd of 3-ch at beg of round, then turn.

Round 6 (RS) Ch 1, 3 sc in 1-ch corner space, *[1 sc in each of next 2 dc, 1 sc in space between next 2 dc (between two 3-dc groups)] 4 times, 1 sc in each of next 2 dc, 3 sc in next 1-ch corner space; rep from * twice, [1 sc in each of next 2 dc, 1 sc in space between next 2 dc] 4 times, 1 sc in each of next 2 dc, join with a sl st to first sc. Fasten off A.

Small flower square

This square is worked using two colors: A and B. Using A, ch 4 and join with a sl st to first ch to form a ring.

Simple striped square

Bonbon square

Round 1 Ch 1, 8 sc in ring, join with a sl st to first sc.

Round 2 Ch 1, 1 sc in same space where sl st just made, *ch 3, 1 sc in next sc; rep from * 6 times, ch 3, join with a sl st to first sc. *8 3-ch loops made.* Fasten off A.

Round 3 Join B to any sc, *ch 5 (to count as first dc and first 2-ch space), 1 dc in same place as B was joined in, *ch 1, 1 sc in next sc, ch 1, work [1 dc, ch 2, 1 dc] all in next sc; rep from * twice, ch 1, 1 sc in next sc, ch 1, join with a sl st to 3rd of 5-ch at beg of round.

Round 4 Ch 1, 3 sc in next 2-ch space, *[2 sc in next 1-ch space] twice, 3 sc in corner 2-ch space; rep from * twice, [2 sc in next 1-ch space] twice, join with a sl st to first sc. Fasten off B.

Simple striped square

This square is worked using three colors: A, B, and C. Using A, ch 6 and join with a sl st to first ch to form a ring.

Round 1 Ch 3, 2 dc in ring, ch 1, [3 dc in ring, ch 1] 3 times, join with a sl st to 3rd of 3-ch at beg of

round. Fasten off A.

Round 2 Join B to same place as last sl st, ch 3, 1 dc in each of next 2 dc, *work [2 dc, ch 1, 2 dc] all in corner 1-ch space, 1 dc in each of next 3 dc; rep from * twice, work [2 dc, ch 1, 2 dc] all in last corner 1-ch space, join with a sl st to 3rd of 3-ch at beg of round. Fasten off B.

Round 3 Join C to same place as last sl st, ch 3, 1 dc in each of next 4 dc, *work [2 dc, ch 1, 2 dc] all in corner 1-ch space, 1 dc in each of next 7 dc; rep from * twice, work [2 dc, ch 1, 2 dc] in last corner 1-ch space, 1 dc in each of next 2 dc, join with a sl st to 3rd of 3-ch at beg of round. Fasten off C.

Round 3 Join B to same place as last sl st, ch 3, 1 dc in each of next 6 dc, *work [2 dc, ch 1, 2 dc] all in corner 1-ch space, 1 dc in each of next 11 dc; rep from * twice, work [2 dc, ch 1, 2 dc] in last corner 1-ch space, 1 dc in each of next 4 dc, join with a sl st to 3rd of 3-ch at beg of round. Fasten off B.

Note: To make square bigger, change colors on every round and continue as set, working 1 dc in each dc and [2 dc, ch 1, 2 dc] in each corner on each round.

Bonbon square

This square is worked using four colors: A, B, C, and D. Using A, make a drawstring ring (see page 82) and begin rounds as follows:

Round 1 Insert hook through ring, yo and draw a loop through ring, then work ch 3, 11 dc in ring, pull yarn tail to close ring and join with a sl st to 3rd of 3-ch at beg of round. *12 sts.* Fasten off A.

Round 2 Join B to same place as last sl st, ch 3, 1 dc in same place as B was joined in, *2 dc in next dc; rep from * to end of round, join with a sl st to 3rd of 3-ch at beg of round. *24 sts.* Fasten off B.

Round 3 Join C to same place as last sl st, ch 1, 1 sc in same place as C was joined in, 2 sc in next dc, *1 sc in next dc, 2 sc in next dc; rep from * to end of round, join with a sl st to 3rd of 3-ch at beg of round. *36 sts.* Fasten off C.

Round 4 Join D to same place as last sl st, ch 4, 4 tr in same place as D was joined in, *1 dc in next dc, 1 hdc in each of next 6 dc, 1 dc in next dc, 5 tr in next dc; rep from * twice, 1 dc in next dc, 1 hdc in each of next 6 dc, 1 dc in next dc, join with a sl st to 4th of 4-ch at beg of round.

Round 5 Ch 3, 1 dc in same place as last sl st, 1 dc in next st, 5 dc in corner tr (center tr of 5-tr group), *1 dc in each of next 12 sts, 5 dc in next corner tr; rep from * twice, 1 dc in each of last 10 sts, join with a sl st to 3rd of 3-ch at beg of round. Fasten off D.

Afghan pentagon (see page 100)

This motif is worked using three colors: A, B, and C. Using A, ch 5 and join with a sl st to first ch to form a ring.

Round 1 Ch 3, 1 dc in ring, *ch 1, 2 dc in ring; rep from * 3 times, ch 1, join with a sl st to 3rd of 3-ch at beg of round. *5 1-ch spaces.* Fasten off A.

Round 2 Join B to any 1-ch space, ch 3, work [1 dc, ch 1 (to form first corner), 2 dc] all in same 1-ch space, ch 1, *work [2 dc, ch 1 (to form next corner), 2 dc] all in next 1-ch space, ch 1; rep from * 3 times, join with a sl st to 3rd of 3-ch at beg of round. Fasten off B.

Round 3 Join C to 1-ch space of any corner, ch 3, work [1 tr, ch 1 (to form first corner), 2 dc] all in same 1-ch space, *ch 1, 2 dc in next 1-ch space (between corners), ch 1, work [2 dc, ch 1 (to form next corner), 2 dc] all in next 1-ch space of next corner; rep from * 3 times, ch 1, 2 dc in next 1-ch space, ch 1, join with a sl st to 3rd of 3-ch at beg of round. Fasten off C.

Round 4 Join B to 1-ch space of any corner, ch 1, 2 sc in same space as 1-ch, then *work 1 sc in each dc and each 1-ch space to next 1-ch space of next corner, 2 sc in corner space; rep from * to end, join with a sl st to first sc. Fasten off B.

Round 5 Join C to first sc of any 2-sc group at a corner, ch 1, 2 sc in same place as 1-ch, 1 sc in each sc to next 2-sc group at next corner, *2 sc in next sc, 1 sc in each sc to next 2-sc group at corner; rep from * to end, join with a sl st to first sc. Fasten off C.

Troubleshooting tips

• Although afghan squares are traditionally worked in wool yarns, they can look great worked in cotton or mohair yarns.

• Keep your motif experiments for future reference and tag them, making a note of the yarn and hook size used.

• When joining new colors onto a motif, don't forget to work over the yarn ends to avoid having to darn them in later.

Afghan pentagon

Striped octagon

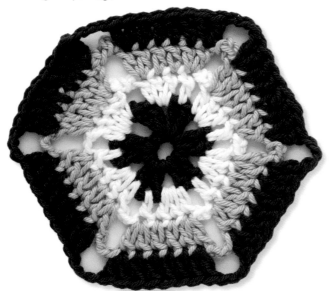

Spoked hexagon

Lacy octagon

Striped octagon

This motif is worked using 3 colors: A, B, and C.

Using A, ch 4 and join with a sl st to first ch to form a ring.

Round 1 Ch 3 (to count as first hdc and first 1-ch space), *1 hdc in ring, ch 1; rep from * 6 times, join with a sl st to 2nd of 3-ch at beg of round. *8 1-ch spaces.*

Round 2 Ch 2, work [1 hdc, ch 1, 1 hdc] all in first 1-ch space, *1 hdc in next hdc, work [1 hdc, ch 1, 1 hdc] all in next 1-ch space; rep from * to end, join with a sl st to 2nd of 2-ch at beg of round. Fasten off A.

Round 3 Join B to first hdc after any 1-ch space, ch 2,

1 hdc in each of next 2 hdc, work [1 hdc, ch 1, 1 hdc] all in next 1-ch space, *1 hdc in each of next 3 hdc, work [1 hdc, ch 1, 1 hdc] all in next 1-ch space; rep from * to end, join with a sl st to 2nd of 2-ch at beg of round. Fasten off B.

Round 4 Join A to first hdc after any 1-ch space, ch 2, 1 hdc in each of next 4 hdc, work [1 hdc, ch 1, 1 hdc] all in next 1-ch space, *1 hdc in each of next 5 hdc, work [1 hdc, ch 1, 1 hdc] all in next 1-ch space; rep from * to end, join with a sl st to 2nd of 2-ch at beg of round. Fasten off A.

Round 5 Join C to first hdc after any 1-ch space, ch 2, 1 hdc in each of next 6 hdc, *2 dc in next 1-ch space, 1 dc in each of next 7 hdc; rep from * to end, 2 dc in last 1-ch space, join with a sl st to 2nd of 2-ch at beg of round. Fasten off C.

Spoked hexagon

This motif is worked using three colors: A, B, and C. Using A, ch 5 and join with a sl st to first ch to form a ring.

Round 1 Ch 4, [2 dc, ch 1] 5 times in ring, 1 dc in ring, join with a sl st to 3rd of 4-ch at beg of round. Fasten off A.

Round 2 Join B to same place as last sl st, ch 3, *2 dc in next 1-ch space, 1 dc in next dc, ch 2, 1 dc in next dc; rep from * 4 times, 2 dc in next 1-ch space, 1 dc in next dc, ch 2, join with a sl st to 3rd of 3-ch at beg of round. Fasten off B.

Round 3 Join C to same place as last sl st, ch 3, 1 dc in same place as 3-ch, *1 dc in each of next 2 dc, 2 dc in next dc, ch 3, 2 dc in next dc; rep from * 4 times, 1 dc in each of next 2 dc, 2 dc in next dc, ch 3, join with a sl st to 3rd of 3-ch at beg of round. Fasten off C.

Round 4 Join in A to same place as last sl st, ch 3, 1 dc in same place as 3-ch, *1 dc in each of next 4 dc, 2 dc in next dc, ch 3, 2 dc in next dc; rep from * 4 times, 1 dc each of next 4 dc, 2 dc in next dc, ch 3, join with a sl st to 3rd of 3-ch at beg of round. Fasten off A.

Lacy octagon

This motif is worked using three colors: A, B, and C. Using A, ch 6 and join with a sl st to first ch to form a ring.

Round 1 Ch 3, work 23 dc in ring, join with a sl st to 3rd of 3-ch at beg of round. *24 sts.*

Round 2 Ch 5, 1 dc in same place as 5-ch, ch 1, *skip 2 dc, work [1 dc, ch 2, 1 dc] all in next dc, ch 1; rep from * 6 times, join with a sl st to 3rd of 5-ch at beg of round. Fasten off A.

Round 3 Join B to any 1-ch space, ch 3, *work [2 dc, ch 2, 2 dc] all in next 2-ch space, 1 dc in next 1-ch space; rep from * 6 times, work [2 dc, ch 2, 2 dc] all in last 2-ch space, join with a sl st to 3rd of 3-ch at beg of round. Fasten off B.

Round 4 Join C to any 2-ch space, ch 1, 2 sc in same space as 1-ch, *1 sc in each of next 5 dc, 2 sc in next 2-ch space; rep from * 6 times more, 1 sc in each of last 5 dc, join with a sl st to first sc. Fasten off C.

Troubleshooting tips

- While you are crocheting a motif—especially a many-sided one—don't worry if the shape doesn't seem to have perfect corners; blocking the finished motif will do the trick. Smooth out the motif when blocking and place a pin at each corner to make the corners more pronounced. Press the motif lightly if the yarn-care instructions indicate the yarn can be pressed, or wet block it (see page 15).

- If you are making an afghan throw with motifs in many colors, arrange the motifs on the floor before stitching them together so that you achieve the best possible color composition.

Wagon wheel throw

This throw is made up of 188 hexagon motifs. It might sound daunting, but each motif is worked in just two simple rounds, which makes it a great project for beginners!

If a subdued color palette is not to your liking, you can choose any four colors to replace those used here. You could also economize by using left-over balls of yarn plus some new ones to make a multicolored mixture. When sewing together hexagons made with your personal choice of shades, use the most neutral shade for the seams.

Size
The finished throw measures approximately 39½in (100cm) by 53¼in (135cm).

What you need
Rowan *Handknit Cotton* in four colors as follows:

A	Ecru (251)	5 x 1¾oz/50g balls
B	Raffia (330)	5 x 1¾oz/50g balls
C	Chime (204)	4 x 1¾oz/50g balls
D	Linen (205)	5 x 1¾oz/50g balls

Size G-6 (4mm) crochet hook
Blunt-ended yarn needle

Gauge
Each hexagon measures 3½in (9cm) from one corner to opposite corner an 4in (10cm) from one straight side to opposite side using a size G-6 (4mm) hook *or size necessary to obtain correct gauge*.

Abbreviations
See page 13.

Wagon wheel hexagon motif
Using size G-6 (4mm) hook and desired shade (see instructions for throw), ch 6 and join with a sl st to first ch to form a ring.

Round 1 Ch 6, *1 tr in ring, ch 2; rep from * 10 times more, join with a sl st to 4th of 6-ch at beg of round. *12 2-ch spaces.*

Round 2 1 sl st in next ch sp (center of first 2-ch space), ch 3, work [1 dc, ch 2, 2 dc] all in same space (to form first corner of hexagon), 3 dc in next 2-ch space, *work [2 dc, ch 2, 2 dc] all in next 2-ch space (to form next corner of hexagon), 3 dc in next 2-ch space; rep from * to end, join with a sl st to 3rd of 3-ch at beg of round. *6 corners made.* Fasten off.

To make throw
Following the instructions for the Wagon Wheel Hexagon, make 49 hexagons in A, 49 in B, 45 in C, and 45 in D.

Finishing
Block and press hexagons into shape (see page 15). Use a blunt-ended yarn needle and C to sew all shapes together as follows:

Take seven hexagons in A and seven in B (a total of 14 hexagons), and sew them together to form a strip, starting with a hexagon in A and alternating the colors. Make six more strips with A and B in this way (a total of seven strips).

Take eight hexagons in C and seven in D (a total of 15 hexagons), and sew them together to form a strip, starting and ending with a hexagon in C. Make two more strips in this way (a total of three strips).

Take seven hexagons in C and eight in D (a total of 15 hexagons), and sew them together to form a strip, starting and ending with a hexagon in D. Make two more strips in this way (a total of three strips).

Sew the prepared strips together, starting and ending with an A/B strip and alternating A/B strips, with C/D strips and D/C strips as shown.

Darn in any yarn ends.

workshop
four

Creating crochet textures

In Workshop Four you will first look at different ways of creating texture in crochet, starting with variations on the basic stitches that you have already mastered and then moving on to fancy stitches, which give a more decorative texture effect. After experimenting with these textures, you can try out lace and filet crochet, and finally crochet colorwork.

Up until now you have worked stitches into the top of the stitches of the previous row, but this workshop shows how varying the place into which you insert the hook will create a variety of stitch patterns and textures. Some of these stitches are perfect for bags and hats, due to their compact structure, while others are just right for shawls and scarves as they drape so well. Make small swatches to decide which yarn and stitch is right for your personal designs.

Simple texture techniques

There are all kinds of crochet stitches that can be used to create texture. Those shown here are variations on the basic crochet stitches that you have already learned. They are fairly compact and most are suitable for making bags or hats.

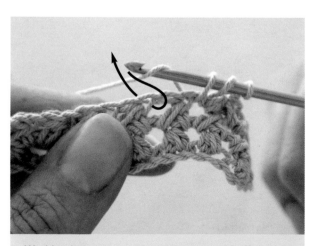

Working into spaces to create crossed half doubles

A few of the most common simple texture techniques are introduced below and on the three following pages. The steps explain how to work stitches in a space between stitches, around the post of a stitch, and into either the front or back loop of the top of a stitch—all of which produce unique surface textures unlike the plain basic crochet stitches.

Working into spaces

You have already learned how to work into a "space" when starting the center of an afghan motif where the first round is work into the central foundation ring. Instead of inserting the hook through the loop of a stitch, you insert it through an open "space."

The Crossed Half Doubles stitch pattern is a good example of this texture technique (see arrow). Each "arm" of each "crossed half double" is worked into a chain space of the previous row so that the stitch sits directly above the stitch in the row below. Try the stitch following the pattern on page 110–111.

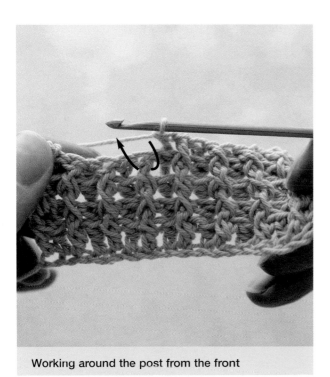

Working around the post from the front

Working around the post from the back

Creating raised/indented textures

By working around the post (or stem) of a tall stitch you can create raised or indented surfaces in the crochet fabric. These stitches are sometimes referred to a "raised stitches," or half doubles or doubles "in relief."

The rib-like texture of the samples on this page is achieved by crocheting half double crochet stitches "around the post from the front" and "around the post from the back" alternately across each row. Begin by making a foundation chain of an even number of stitches and working the first row in double crochet. Work the second row as explained below.

Working around the post from the front

Start the second row with two chains. Then wrap the yarn around the hook and insert your hook *from the front* of the work around the stem of the first stitch in the previous row as shown by the path of the arrow. Yarn over hook and draw a loop through. Yarn over hook and draw through all three loops on the hook to complete the raised half double. This technique pushes the stitch below forward to give a raised effect.

Working around the post from the back

To begin the second stitch in the second row, wrap the yarn around the hook and insert your hook *from the back* around the stem of next stitch in the previous row as shown by the path of the arrow. Yarn over hook and draw a loop through. Yarn over hook and draw through all three loops on the hook to complete the raised half double. This technique pushes the stitch below backward to give an indented appearance. Continue working around the post from the front and the back alternately to the end of the row.

To achieve the all-over reversible rib texture in the photograph, work matching raised and indented stitches on all the following rows.

Inserting the hook through the front loop

Working into the front loops on every row

Creating ridged effects

Ridged patterns are a very effective way of creating texture in crochet. The ridges (or ribs) run horizontally across the crochet fabric, rather than vertically like raised stitches (see page 107). The technique used is a simple one—you work into only one side of the top of the stitch below. This is called "working into the front of the stitch" or "working into the back of the stitch." It is very important to learn this technique as it is used in combination with other stitches in many crochet patterns.

Look at the top edge of your crochet. The stitches look like the links of a chain: there is one loop at the front of the stitch and one at the back. A different effect is produced depending on whether you work through both loops at once, or into either only the front or the back of the stitch. Your pattern will always tell you if you should work only into the front or back of a stitch; if it doesn't mention what to do, always work through both loops as you learned for the basic stitches in Workshop One.

Working into the front loops

To try out a simple ridged stitch, work one row of single crochet. Then follow these steps starting with the second row.

1 Begin the second row with one chain as usual. Then insert your hook *into the front loop only* of the first stitch (see arrow), rather than through the whole top of the stitch, and complete the single crochet. Work each single crochet of the row in this way.

2 Work the following rows as for row 2, working all the stitches into the front loop only of each stitch. This creates a slightly raised ridge running across the work below every other row, and both sides of the crochet look exactly the same.

Working into the back loops

Working single crochet into the back loop of each stitch creates a much more pronounced effect than working into the front loop.

Begin by working a row of single crochet, then turn the work and follow these steps.

1 Start the second row with one chain in the usual way. Next, insert your hook *into the back loop only* of the first stitch, rather than through the whole top of the stitch, and complete the single crochet. Work each single crochet to the end of the row in the same way, inserting the hook each time through the back loop only of the stitch in the row below.

2 Work the following rows as for row 2, working all the stitches into the back loop only of each stitch. This creates a recessed ridge running across the work on every other row, and a deeper texture than when you work into the front loops only. (The pattern for this, called Ridge Stitch, is given on page 110.)

Inserting the hook through the back loop

Working into the back loops on every row

Troubleshooting tips

- Textured stitches show off their attributes better if you work them in smooth yarns that will accentuate the textures and not hide them.

- Work your simple texture swatches with different hook sizes to see what effect this has on their appearance.

- Keep all your stitch pattern swatches together in a box and make sure they are labeled so you that you know what book you found them in, and on which page!

Simple texture patterns

The following patterns offer a variety of easy-to-work subtle crochet textures. Detailed instructions for the techniques used for Crossed Half Doubles, Rib Stitch, and Ridge Stitch are provided on pages 106–109.

With the exception of Rib Stitch, all of these stitch patterns look exactly the same on both sides, which makes them perfect for items that need to be reversible, such as scarves and throws.

Up and down stitch

Make an odd number of ch.

Row 1 1 dc in 3rd ch from hook, *1 sc next ch, 1 dc in next ch; rep from * to end, turn.

Row 2 Ch 2, skip first dc, *1 dc in next sc, 1 sc in next dc; rep from * to end, 1 dc in 2nd of 2-ch, turn.

Rep row 2 to form pattern.

Ridge stitch

Make any number of ch.

Row 1 1 sc in 2nd ch from hook, 1 sc in each of rem ch to end, turn.

Row 2 Ch 1, then working into back loop only of top of each st, work 1 sc in each sc to end, turn.

Rep row 2 to form pattern.

Cable stitch

Make a multiple of 4 ch plus 2.

Row 1 1 sc in 2nd ch from hook, 1 sc in each of rem ch, turn.

Row 2 Ch 3, *skip next sc, 1 dc in each of next 3 sc, yo, insert hook from front to back in last sc skipped and work a dc; rep from * to end, 1 dc in last sc, turn.

Row 3 Ch 1, skip first dc, 1 sc in each dc to end, 1 sc in 3rd of 3-ch, turn.

Rep rows 2 and 3 to form pattern.

Alternate stitch

Make an odd number of ch.

Row 1 2 sc in 3rd ch from hook, *skip 1 ch, 2 sc in next ch; rep from * to end, turn.

Row 2 Ch 2, skip first sc, 2 sc in next sc, *skip next sc, 2 sc in next sc; rep from * to end, turn.

Rep row 2 to form pattern.

Rib stitch

Make a multiple of 2 ch plus 4.

Row 1 (RS) 1 dc in 4th ch from hook, 1 dc in each of rem ch, turn

Row 2 Ch 1, 1 sc in each dc to end, 1 sc in top of t-ch, turn.

Row 3 Ch 2, inserting hook from front to back and to front again around 3-ch at beg of row 1, work 1 raised hdc from the front around these ch, skip first sc, 1 sc in next sc, *skip next sc of row 2 and work 1 raised hdc from the front around post of dc of row 1 (below skipped st), 1 sc in next sc of row 2; rep from * to end, turn.

Row 4 Ch 1, *1 sc in top of each sc and each raised hdc to end, turn.

Row 5 Ch 2, 1 raised hdc from the front around post of first raised hdc 2 rows below, skip first sc, 1 sc in next sc, *1 raised hdc from the front around post of next raised hdc 2 rows below, skip 1 sc, 1 sc in next sc; rep from * to end, turn.

Rep rows 4 and 5 to form pattern.

Crossed half doubles

Make an odd number of ch.

Row 1 Yo, insert hook in 3rd ch from hook, yo and draw a loop through, yo, insert hook in next ch, yo and draw a loop through, yo and draw through all

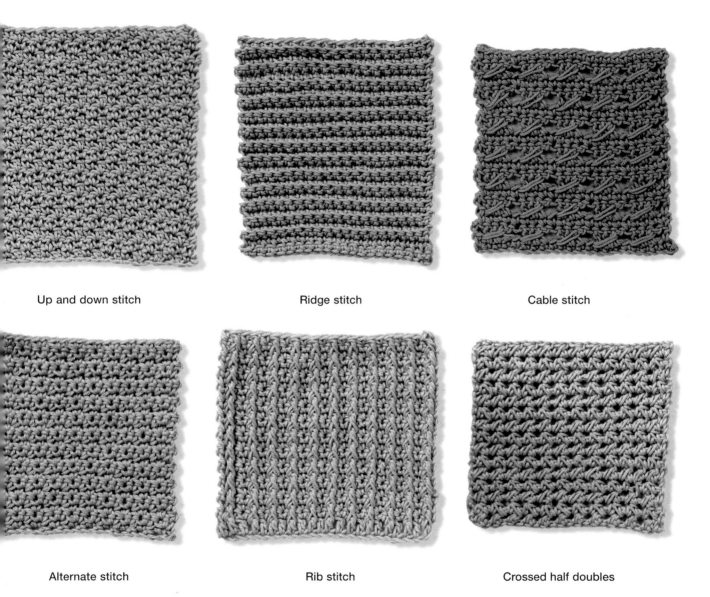

Up and down stitch

Ridge stitch

Cable stitch

Alternate stitch

Rib stitch

Crossed half doubles

5 loops on hook (to complete first crossed half double), ch 1, *[yo, insert hook in next ch, yo and draw a loop through] twice, yo and draw through all 5 loops on hook (to complete next crossed half double), ch 1; rep from * to last ch, 1 hdc in last ch, turn.
Row 2 Ch 2, yo, insert hook in first ch sp, yo and draw a loop through, yo, insert hook in next ch sp, yo and draw a loop through, yo and draw through all

5 loops on hook, ch 1, *yo, insert hook in same ch sp as 2nd arm of last crossed half double, yo and draw a loop through, yo, insert hook in next ch sp, yo and draw a loop through, yo and draw through all 5 loops on hook, ch 1; rep from * to end (working 2nd arm of last crossed half double in ch sp formed by t-ch), 1 hdc in 2nd of 2-ch, turn.
Rep row 2 to form pattern.

Decorative texture techniques

Fancy crochet stitches can be used to create a variety of unusual and exciting textures. Some are made by forming "clusters" or by working loops or stitches in the spaces of the preceding row, or a combination of these. There are many variations on these basic methods, and here are just a few examples.

Pineapple stitch

This stitch is created by working into the spaces in the row below, rather than into the tops of stitches.

To work Pineapple Stitch, follow the instructions on page 114. Each "pineapple" is made by working the first loops of four half double crochet stitches into a chain space and then joining the tops of the stitches together as shown by the arrow.

Bobble stitch

In this stitch, single crochet stitches are worked between the tall stitches of the bobbles to create the raised effect.

Follow the pattern on page 114 to work Bobble Stitch. The bobbles are worked on the wrong-side rows so that they stick out at the front. Each bobble is made up of five partially worked doubles that are joined together at the top as shown by the arrow.

Starburst stitch

The so-called "starburst" effect is created by joining a number of stitches together at the top in one row and then working a number of stitches fanning out from the center of the joined stitches in the next row.

Here, the first two rows have been worked following the pattern on page 114. In the next row a fan of double crochet stitches is worked into the center (see arrow) of the clustered stitches of the previous row.

Pineapple stitch—joining the stitches together

Bobble stitch—closing the top of the bobble

Starburst stitch—working a fan of stitches

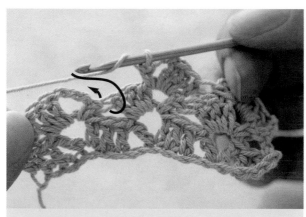

Brick stitch—working into the chain space

Brick stitch

In brick stitch, the stitches are staggered from row to row. The texture is created by working groups of stitches into the chain spaces of the row below.

Try the stitch following the instructions on page 114. The brick-like effect is achieved by working three double crochet stitches, three chains, and one single crochet all into each chain space (see arrow) of the row below. The three chains and the single crochet make the groups of doubles tilt to the right. Each row is worked in the same way, so the "bricks" tilt in a different direction from row to row.

Loop stitch

Loop stitch produces a fun texture of masses of long loops on the right side of the crochet. It takes a little practice because you have to keep the loop on your finger while you work off the loops on the hook.

Follow the instructions on page 115 to crochet the loop stitch pattern, but work the first few loops as described by the steps here. They show you how to make the individual loops, which are worked on every other row between rows of single crochet. If you find you have trouble keeping all the loops similar in length, you can wrap them around a width of cardboard instead of your finger.

Loop stitch—making a loop

1 With the wrong side of the work facing, wrap the yarn around your left index finger to create a loop of the desired size. Then insert the hook through the first single crochet and behind the yarn on your index finger (see arrow). Keeping your finger in the loop to maintain its size, draw both strands of the loop through the single crochet so that you have three loops on the hook.

Loop stitch—anchoring the loop

2 Drop the loop from your index finger. Yarn over hook and draw a loop through all three loops on the hook (see arrow) to complete the loop.

Decorative texture patterns

These texture stitches are just a few of the many popular fancy crochet stitches that are available in crochet stitch pattern books. See pages 112–113 for a explanation of some of the techniques used here.

Pineapple stitch

Make a multiple of 2 ch plus 4.

Row 1 Yo, insert hook in 4th ch from hook, yo and draw a lp through, [yo, insert hook, yo and draw a lp through] 3 times all in same ch (4th ch from hook), yo and draw through first 8 lps on hook, yo and draw through rem 2 lps, ch 1, *skip 1 ch, [yo, insert hook, yo and draw a lp through] 4 times all in next ch, yo and draw through first 8 lps on hook, yo and draw through rem 2 lps, ch 1; rep from *to last 2 ch, skip 1 ch, 1 dc in last ch, turn.

Row 2 Ch 3, *[yo, insert hook, yo and draw a lp through] 4 times all in next ch sp, yo and draw through first 8 lps on hook, yo and draw through rem 2 lps, ch 1; rep from * to end, 1 dc in top of t-ch, turn.

Rep row 2 to form pattern.

Bobble stitch

Make a multiple of 3 ch plus 2.

Row 1 (RS) 1 sc in 2nd ch from hook, 1 sc in each of rem ch, turn.

Row 2 (WS) Ch 1, in first sc work [yo, insert hook, yo and draw a lp through, yo and draw through 2 lps on hook] 5 times, yo and draw through all 6 lps on hook—called *1 bobble*—, *1 sc in each of next 2 sc, 1 bobble in next sc; rep from * to end, turn.

Row 3 Ch 1, 1 sc in each bobble and each sc, turn.

Row 4 Ch 1, *1 sc in each of next 2 sc, 1 bobble in next sc; rep from * to last sc, 1 sc in last sc, turn.

Row 5 Rep row 3.

Row 6 Ch 1, 1 sc in first sc, *1 bobble in next sc, 1 sc

in each of next 2 sc; rep from * to end, turn.

Row 7 Rep row 3.

Rep rows 2–7 to form pattern.

Brick stitch

Make a multiple of 4 ch plus 2.

Row 1 1 dc in 4th ch from hook, 1 dc in next ch, [1 dc, ch 3, 1 dc] all in next ch, *skip 1 ch, 1 dc in each of next 2 ch, [1 dc, ch 3, 1 dc] all in next ch; rep from * to last 4 ch, skip 1 ch, 1 dc in each of last 3 ch, turn.

Row 2 Ch 3, [3 dc, ch 3, 1 sc] all in each 3-ch sp to end, 1 dc between last group of 3-dc and t-ch, turn.

Rep row 2 to form pattern.

Starburst stitch

Make a multiple of 8 ch plus 2.

Row 1 1 sc in 2nd ch from hook, *skip 3 ch, 9 dc in next ch, skip 3 ch, 1 sc in next ch; rep from * to end, turn.

Row 2 Ch 3, skip first st, work a 4-dc cluster over next 4 sts by working [yo, insert hook, yo and draw a lp through, yo and draw through 2 lps on hook] in each st, yo and draw through all 5 lps on hook to complete cluster, *ch 4, 1 sc in next st, ch 3, 9-dc cluster over next 9 sts; rep from *, ending with ch 4, 1 sc in next st, ch 3, 5-dc cluster, turn.

Row 3 Ch 4, 4 dc in top of 5-dc cluster, 1 sc in sc, *9 dc in top of 9-dc cluster, 1 sc in sc; rep from *, ending with 5 dc in top of 4-dc cluster, turn.

Row 4 Ch 3, skip 1 dc, *9-dc cluster, ch 4, 1 sc in next dc, ch 3; rep from *, ending with 1 sc in top of t-ch, turn.

Row 5 Ch 1, 1 sc in first sc, *9 dc in top of 9-dc cluster, 1 sc in sc; rep from *, ending with 1 sc in first of t-ch, turn.

Rep rows 2–5 to form pattern.

Pineapple stitch

Bobble stitch

Brick stitch

Starburst stitch

Loop stitch

Make any number of ch.

Row 1 1 sc in 2nd ch from hook, 1 sc in each of rem ch, turn.

Row 2 (WS) Ch 1 (does NOT count as first st), *wrap yarn around left index finger, insert hook in next sc and around behind both strands of loop on finger, draw both strands through sc, yo and draw a lp through all 3 lps on hook; rep from * to end, turn.

Row 3 Ch 1, 1 sc in each st to end, turn.

Rep rows 2–3 to form pattern.

Loop stitch

Lace and filet crochet

Openwork lace and filet crochet are both worked using combinations of basic stitches spaced apart with chains. Lace stitches are a more open version of the fancy stitches shown on pages 112–115, whereas filet crochet relies on a simple mesh, in which stitches can be filled in or left open to create a pattern. To slowly gain confidence with openwork crochet, start out with simple filet crochet before attempting the more complicated Solomon's knot and then the lace patterns on pages 120–121.

Filet crochet

Filet crochet is the easiest to work of all the openwork crochet stitches. The technique is based on a mesh of squares made with double crochet stitches and chains. Patterns are built up on the mesh by leaving some squares empty and filling in others. Once you learn how to make the basic filet mesh and the filled in mesh, you can follow any filet chart without having to read row-by-row instructions.

Working the basic filet mesh

To start the mesh, make a multiple of 2 chains, plus 5 extra. On the first row begin by working 1 double crochet in the 7th chain from the hook, then *chain 1, skip the next chain and work 1 double in the next chain; repeat from * to the end of the chain.

Turn and begin the second row with chain 4, then work 1 double in the first double, *chain 1, 1 double in the next double (see arrow right); repeat from *, working the last double in the top of the turning chain.

Work the following rows of the basic filet mesh in the same way as the second row, starting every row with chain 4 and working the last double into the third of the 4 turning chains.

Working blocks and spaces

The open squares of the filet mesh are called filet "spaces." Patterns are formed on the mesh by filling in some of the open squares with doubles; these filled in squares are called filet "blocks."

To make a block over a space, instead of working a chain over the top of the one-chain space below, work a double into it. To work blocks over blocks, simply work a double into each double. To work a space over a block, chain 1 and skip the double below it.

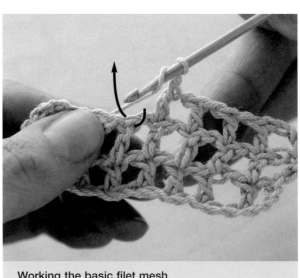

Working the basic filet mesh

Flower filet chart

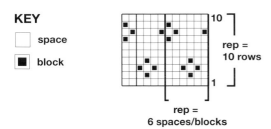

KEY

☐ space

■ block

rep =
10 rows

rep =
6 spaces/blocks

Working filet crochet from charts

Once you have practised making filet spaces and blocks you are ready to follow a filet pattern chart. The chart above is for the sample on the right.

The empty squares on the chart represent spaces and the filled in square represent blocks, as indicated by the key that always accompanies a filet chart. Start by making a foundation chain of two chains for every space you want to make in your first row, then work five extra chains (for the side edge). Work the first row of spaces as explained on the opposite page.

Make the pattern as shown on the chart, reading the odd-numbered rows from right to left and the even-numbered rows from left to right, and repeating the 6-space/block repeat as many times as you like.

Filet crochet in symbols

If you are having difficulties understanding how the blocks and spaces are formed on filet crochet, look at the symbol diagram below (see page 13 for symbols). It illustrates exactly how they are made.

Filet in symbols

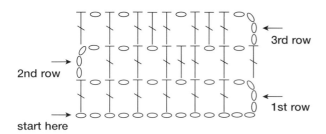

3rd row

2nd row

1st row

start here

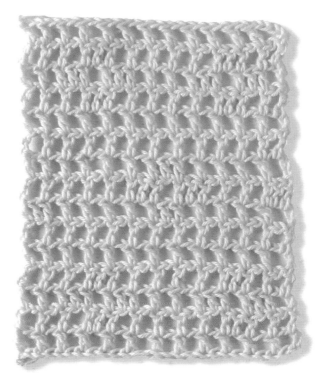

Flower filet pattern

Troubleshooting tips

• A good source of patterns for filet crochet are simple cross-stitch motifs. You can plan your repeats by making your own chart on graph paper.

• The basic filet mesh given on these pages uses "spaces" one chain wide and "blocks" three stitches wide, which works well for lightweight and medium-weight yarns. But if you want to work filet with a very fine thread and hook, try the traditional filet, which uses "spaces" two chains wide and "blocks" four doubles wide—the technique is exactly the same.

Solomon's knot

Solomon's knot stitch forms an attractive, sturdy mesh that looks great when worked in string for a bag, or in a fine mohair for a shawl. No foundation chain is required—instead, a row of Solomon's Knot stitches form the foundation.

A standard extended loop length for Solomon's Knot is ½–⅝in (12–15mm). Measure your first few loops and after a while you will find that you can judge the loop length by eye. Make a longer loop for a thicker yarn and a shorter one for fine yarn, but try to keep the length consistent within the piece.

The pattern instructions for working Solomon's knot are given on the next page, but follow the step-by-step instructions to learn the basics.

Working the stitch step by step

1 Begin with a slip knot on the hook (here the first two Solomon's knots have been completed to show the basic stitch). To begin each stitch, extend the loop on the hook to about about ⅝in (15mm) long. Yo and draw a loop through the extended loop as shown by the arrow.

2 Insert the hook between the double and single strands of the extended loop (see arrow). Yo and draw a loop through.

3 Yo and draw through both the loops on the hook to complete the knot. Work an even number of knots in the same way to complete the first row.

4 To begin the second row, skip the knot on the hook and the next 3 knots, and work 1 sc in the next knot as shown by the arrow.

5 Follow the pattern instructions (see next page) to complete row 2 and continue the stitch.

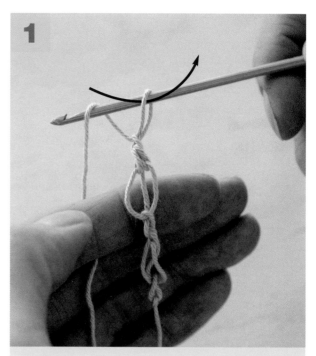

Drawing a loop through the extended loop

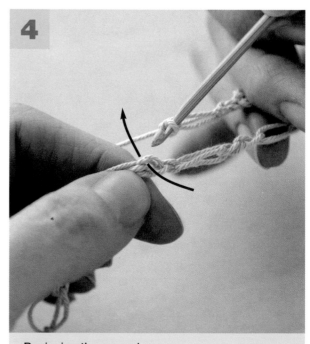

Beginning the second row

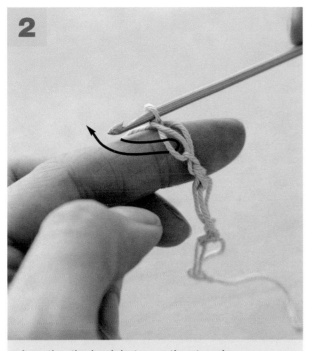

Inserting the hook between the strands

Completing the knot

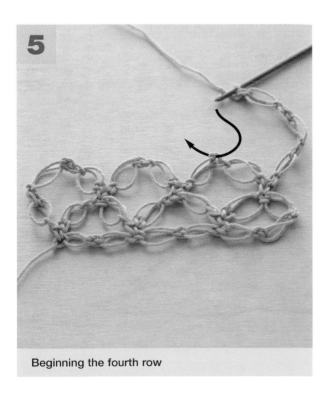

Beginning the fourth row

Solomon's knot pattern

Referring to the steps for making the knots, follow this pattern to work Solomon's knot:

Make a slip knot and place it on hook.

Row 1 *Extend loop on hook to ½in (12mm) long, yo and draw a loop through loop on hook, insert hook between double and single strands of extended loop just made, yo and draw a loop through, yo and draw though both loops on hook to complete knot; rep from * for length required (making an even number of knots in total), turn.

Row 2 Skip knot on hook and next 3 knots, 1 sc in next knot, *make 2 knots (as explained in row 1), skip next knot in row 1, 1 sc in next knot; rep from * to end, working last sc in first ch in row 1, turn.

Row 3 Make 3 knots, 1 sc in next free knot in previous row, *make 2 knots, 1 sc in next free knot in previous row; rep from * to end, turn.

Rep row 3 to form pattern.

Lace patterns

Crochet lace was traditionally made with fine thread and hooks, but it looks equally effective worked in today's cotton yarns. If you like the few simple lace patterns here, you'll be able to find many more to choose from in crochet stitch pattern books.

Two lace medallions patterns are given here as well. They are worked in the round and can be used to create wonderfully airy throws, delicate pillow covers, or insertions in denser crochet garments. They also make great Christmas decorations if sugar-starched when completed.

Open checks

Make a multiple of 6 ch plus 3.

Row 1 1 dc in 4th ch from hook, 1 dc in next ch, *ch 3, skip 3 ch, 1 dc in each of next 3 ch; rep from * to last 4 ch, ch 3, skip 3 ch, 1 dc in last ch, turn.

Row 2 Ch 3, 2 dc in first 3-ch sp, *ch 3, 3 dc in next 3-ch sp; rep from * to end, ending with ch 3, 1 dc in top of t-ch, turn.

Rep row 2 to form pattern.

Lacy scallops

Make a multiple of 6 ch plus 4.

Row 1 Work [2 dc, ch 3, 2 dc] all in 6th ch from hook, *skip 5 ch, work [2 dc, ch 3, 2 dc] all in next ch; rep from * to last 4 ch, skip 3 ch, 1 dc in last ch, turn.

Row 2 Ch 3, *work [2 dc, ch 3, 2 dc] all in next 3-ch sp; rep from * to end, 1 dc in top of t-ch, turn.

Rep row 2 to form pattern.

Fan stitch

Make a multiple of 14 ch plus 2.

Row 1 1 sc in 2nd ch from hook, *skip 6 ch, work 13 *long-dc* by working [yo, insert hook, yo and draw through a lp ⅝in (1.5cm) long, yo and draw through 2 lps on hook, yo and draw through 2 lps on hook] 13 times all in next ch, skip 6 ch, 1 sc in next ch; rep from * to end, turn.

Row 2 Ch 3, 1 long-dc in first sc, *ch 5, 1 sc in 7th of 13 long-dc, ch 5, 2 long-dc in sc between fans; rep from * to last sc, 2 long-dc in last sc, turn.

Row 3 Ch 1, 1 sc between first 2 long-dc, *13 long-dc

Open checks

Lacy scallops

in sc worked at center of fan in previous row, 1 sc between 2 long-dc of previous row; rep from * to end, working last sc between long-dc and t-ch, turn. Rep rows 2–3 to form pattern.

Open daisy medallion

Ch 10 and join with a sl st to first ch to form a ring.
Round 1 (RS) Ch 1, 18 sc in ring, join with sl st to first sc of round.
Round 2 Ch 4 (counts as first tr), holding last lp of each tr on hook work 2 tr in same place as sl st just made, yo and draw through all lps on hook—called *3-tr cluster*—, *ch 10, skip 2 sc, 3-tr cluster in next sc; rep from * to end, ch 10, join with a sl st to first tr cluster made.
Round 3 *Work [3 sc, (ch 3, 3 sc) 3 times] all in next 10-ch lp; rep from * to end.
Round 4 Ch 6, 1 sc in central picot of next "petal" (the 6-ch will be hidden on WS), *ch 11, 1 sc in next central picot; rep from * to end, ch 11, join with a sl st to first sc of round.
Round 5 Ch 1, *11 sc in 11-ch space, ch 3; rep from * to end, join with a sl st to first sc of round. Fasten off.

Mint sorbet medallion

Ch 10 and join with a sl st to first ch to form a ring.
Round 1 Ch 4, 27 tr in ring, join with a sl st to top of 4-ch at beg of round.
Round 2 1 sc in same place as sl st just made, *ch 5, skip 1 st, 1 sc in next st; rep from * to end, ending with ch 1, 1 tr in first sc made. *14 loops made.*
Round 3 Ch 4 (counts as first tr), holding last loop of each tr on hook work 3 tr in same lp (lp created by 1-ch and tr of last round), yo and draw through all lps on hook—called *4-tr cluster*—, [ch 7, 4-tr cluster in next lp] 13 times, ch 7, join with a sl st to top of first cluster of round. Fasten off.

Fan stitch

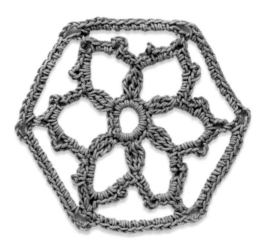

Open daisy medallion

Mint sorbet medallion

Crochet belt

Embellished with crocheted flowers, this lace crochet belt is great fun to make. You can work the belt any length you like and cover it with blooms and leaves to suit your taste. The long and short curlicues on the belt are made with just one row of simple single crochet, which curls naturally if left unpressed.

Size

The finished belt measures approximately 2¼in (6cm) wide by 43¼in (110cm) long or desired length.

What you need

3 x 1¾oz/50g balls of Rowan *Cotton Glace* in desired shade

Sizes D-3 and E-4 (3mm and 3.5mm) crochet hooks

Belt buckle (to be crocheted over), 2¼in (6cm) wide by 2¾in (7cm) tall

Blunt-ended yarn needle

Gauge

Belt pattern measures 2¼in (6cm) across width of belt using size D-3 (3mm) hook *or size to obtain correct gauge.*

Abbreviations

See page 113.

Special note

The numbers of flowers, leaves, bobbles, and curlicues recommended in the instructions are just suggestions. Make more or fewer embellishments if you prefer. They are arranged at random on the belt.

Belt

Using size E-4 (3.5mm) hook, ch 15.

Change to size D-3 (3mm) hook.

Row 1 Work [1 dc, ch 1, 1 dc] all in 5th ch from hook, *skip next 2 ch, work [1 dc, ch 1, 1 dc] all in next ch; rep from * twice, 1 dc in last ch, turn.

Row 2 Ch 3 (to count as first dc), *work [1 dc, ch 1, 1 dc] all in next 1-ch space; rep from * 3 times, 1 dc in top of t-ch, turn.

Rep row 2 until belt is measures 43¼in (110cm) or desired length. Fasten off.

Eight-petal flowers (make 3)

Using size D-3 (3mm) hook, ch 8 and join with a sl st to first ch to make a ring.

Round 1 Ch 1, 16 sc in ring, join with a sl st to first sc.

Round 2 Ch 1 (does NOT count as first st), 1 sc in same place as sl st, ch 5, *skip 1 sc, 1 sc in next sc, ch 5; rep from * to end of round, join with a sl st to first sc. Fasten off.

Seven-petal flowers (make 5)

Using size D-3 (3mm) hook, ch 2.

Round 1 7 sc in 2nd ch from hook, join with a sl st to first sc.

Round 2 Ch 2, work [1 hdc, ch 3, 1 hdc] all in next sc; rep from * 5 times, 1 hdc in same place as sl st at end of previous round, ch 3, join with a sl st to 2nd of 2-ch at beg of round. *7 3-ch spaces made.*

Round 3 1 sl st in next 3-ch space, ch 1, 6 sc in same 3-ch space, 1 sl st in each of next 2 hdc, *6 sc in next 3-ch space, 1 sl st in each of next 2 hdc; rep from * to end of round, join with a sl st to first sc. Fasten off.

Simple daisies (make 5)

Using size D-3 (3mm) hook, ch 4 and join with a with a sl st to first ch to form a ring.

Round 1 Ch 1 (does NOT count as first st), 12 sc in ring, join with a sl st to first sc.

Round 2 Working sts into front loops only of sc of previous round, *ch 4, 1 sl st in same place as last sl st, 1 sl st in next sc; rep from * 11 times. *12 4-ch loops made.*

Round 3 Working sts into back loops only of sc of round 1, ch 3, then work [1 dc, ch 3, 1 sl st] all in same sc as last sl st of round 2, 1 sl st in next sc, *ch 3, work [1 dc, ch 3, 1 sl st] all in same place as last sl st, 1 sl st in next sc; rep from * 10 times. Fasten off.

Leaves (make 11)

Using size D-3 (3mm) hook, ch 9.

Row 1 1 sc in 2nd ch from hook, 1 sc in next ch, 1 hdc in next ch, 1 dc in each of next 2 ch, 1 hdc in next ch, 1 sc in each of last 2 ch, continuing along other side of foundation ch, work 1 sc in each of first 2 ch, 1 hdc in next ch, 1 dc in each of next 2 ch, 1 hdc in next ch, 1 sc in each of last 2 ch. Fasten off.

Bobbles (make 11)

Using size D-3 (3mm) hook, make a drawstring ring (see page 82) and begin rounds as follows:

Round 1 Insert hook through ring and draw a loop through ring, ch 1, 5 sc in ring, pull yarn tail to close ring, place marker (a marker is placed at the end of each round to indicate where each round ends/begins).

Round 2 2 sc in each of next 5 sc, place marker. *10 sc.*

Round 3 1 sc in each of next 10 sc, place marker.

Round 4 *Skip 1 sc, 1 sc in next sc; rep from * to end of round. *5 sc.* Fasten off and remove markers.

Short curlicues (make 14)

Using size D-3 (3mm) hook, ch 7.

Row 1 1 sc in 2nd ch from hook, 1 sc in each of rem ch. *6 sc.* Fasten off.

Long curlicues (make 14)

Using size D-3 (3mm) hook, ch 12.

Row 1 1 sc in 2nd ch from hook, 1 sc in each of rem ch. *11 sc.* Fasten off.

Finishing

Darn in any yarn ends. Press belt and Seven-Petal and Eight-Petal Flowers lightly on wrong side following instructions on yarn label. Do NOT press other pieces.

Buckle

Using size D-3 (3mm) hook, work a row of single crochet around outer edges of belt buckle, pushing sts close together as you proceed so that they completely cover buckle, join with a sl st to first sc made. Fasten off.

Tie yarn to center post of buckle, wind yarn around it to cover it and secure with a few sewn stitches. Wrap foundation-chain end of belt around center post of buckle and sew end to wrong side of belt.

Try belt on for size and determine where you will want belt to sit. Then mark how much of end of belt you need to leave plain in order to thread through belt buckle.

Decoration

Arrange flowers, leaves, curlicues, and bobbles in position at random on belt. Pin then sew them in place.

Troubleshooting tips

- Use any color you like for this belt, or make it multicolored. A black belt with colored flowers and leaves would make a dramatic design.

- The foundation-chain end of the belt is attached to the buckle. This means that you can add rows easily at the other end if you find you need a longer belt—or unravel rows to make it shorter.

Crochet colorwork

You learned how to make simple changes of color from row to row for stripes in Workshop Two, so now you are ready to try your hand at crocheting some decorative stitches, working into spaces and rows below in contrasting colors. After that you can progress to single-crochet jacquard, creating colorwork patterns and motifs by changing the colors within a row. If you have any simple charted cross-stitch and knitting motifs that you love, be sure to try them out here in jacquard crochet.

Colorwork techniques

Wave, Spike, and Almond Stitches are a few of the most popular crochet colorwork stitches. When choosing yarn colors for these stitches, make sure they contrast enough with each other to show off the effects of the stitches. Jacquard crochet is shown here being worked in vertical stripes, but virtually any motif can be crocheted using the technique.

Skipping two stitches at the bottom of the V-shape

Wave stitch

Wave stitch is worked entirely in rows of single crochet. The wave shapes are created by skipping stitches at the bottom of the wave (see top right) and increasing stitches at the pinnacle of the wave.

Work the stitch following the pattern on page 128 and changing color after every two rows.

Spike stitch

Learn the principle of Spike Stitch and you will be able to make up your own pattern using the technique. The overlapping colors and spikes are created by working "extended" single crochet stitches into stitches two rows below (see right). The pattern for this stitch is on page 129.

Working a spike stitch into a stitch two rows below

1 sc in each of first 2 sc, 1 hdc in next sc, 1 dc in each of next 5 sc, 1 hdc in next sc, 1 sc in next sc, *ch 1, skip next sc, 1 sc in next sc, 1 hdc in next sc, 1 dc in each of next 5 sc, 1 hdc in next sc, 1 sc in next sc; rep from * to last sc, 1 sc in last sc, turn.

Row 3 Using B, ch 1, 1 sc in each of first 2 sc, 1 hdc in next hdc, 1 dc in each of next 5 dc, 1 hdc in next hdc, 1 sc in next sc, *ch 1, 1 sc in next sc, 1 hdc in next hdc, 1 dc in each of next 5 dc, 1 hdc in next hdc, 1 sc in next sc; rep from * to last sc, 1 sc in last sc, changing to A with last yo of last sc, turn.

Row 4 Using A, ch 1, 1 sc in each of first 10 sts, *1 dc in skipped sc of row 1, 1 sc in each of next 9 sts; rep from * to last st, 1 sc in last sc, turn.

Row 5 Using A, ch 1, 1 sc in each st to end, changing to B with last yo of last sc, turn.

Row 6 Using B, ch 3 (to count as first dc), skip first sc, 1 dc in each of next 2 sts, *1 hdc in next st, 1 sc in next st, ch 1, skip 1 st, 1 sc in next st, 1 hdc in next st, 1 dc in each of next 5 sts; rep from * to end, but ending with 3 dc instead of 5, turn.

Row 7 Using B, ch 3 (to count as first dc), skip first st, 1 dc in each of next 2 dc, *1 hdc in next hdc, 1 sc in next sc, ch 1, 1 sc in next sc, 1 hdc in next hdc, 1 dc in each of next 5 dc; rep from *to end, but ending with 3 dc instead of 5, working last dc in top of t-ch, and changing to A with last yo of last dc, turn.

Row 8 Using A, ch 1, 1 sc in each of first 5 sts, *1 dc in skipped st of row 5, 1 sc in each of next 9 sts; rep from * to end, but ending with 1 sc in each of next 5 sts, turn.

Row 9 Rep row 5.
Rep rows 2–9 to form pattern.

Spike stitch

This stitch is worked using 3 colors: A, B, and C. Using A, make a multiple of 5 ch.

Row 1 (RS) 1 sc in 2nd ch from hook, 1 sc in each of rem ch, turn.

Row 2 Ch 1 (does NOT count as first st), 1 sc in each sc to end, turn.

Rows 3 and 4 Using B, [rep row 2] twice.

Row 5 Using C, ch 1, 1 sc in each of first 3 sc, *work [1 sc in top of sc 2 rows below next sc, pulling first loop of sc up to same height as other sc of this row—called *1 spike-sc*] 3 times, 1 sc in each of next 2 sc; rep from * to end of row, 1 sc in last sc, turn.

Row 6 Using C, rep row 2.

Rows 7 and 8 Using A, rep rows 5 and 6, but working each spike-sc in row 7 through center of previous spike-sc when working into tops of sts 2 rows below.

Row 9 Using B, ch 1, 1 sc in first sc, *[1 spike-sc in top of sc 2 rows below next sc] twice, 1 sc in each of next 3 sc; rep from * to last 3 sc, [1 spike-sc in top of sc 2 rows below next sc] twice, 1 sc in last sc, turn.

Row 10 Using B, rep row 2.
Rep rows 5–10 to form pattern.

Spike stitch

project **seven**

Felted pots

These projects use many of the skills you will have mastered when you reach this section of the book. To refresh your memory on how to work in the round, turn back to pages 78–83. When working the stripes of the jacquard pattern, remember to change to a new color of yarn with the last "yo" of the previous stitch.

Sizes
Large striped pot: When felted measures 5in (13cm) tall and 4¼in (11cm) in diameter, and has a circumference of 14¼in (36cm).
Medium-size pot with jacquard pattern: When felted measures 4½in (11.5cm) tall and has a circumference of 11¾in (30cm).
Small plain pot: When felted measures 3½in (9cm) tall and has a circumference of 11in (28cm).

What you need
Rowan *Scottish Tweed DK* in three colors as follows:
A   Indigo (013)   2 x 1¾oz/50g balls
B   Autumn (029)   1 x 1¾oz/50g ball
C   Thistle (016)   1 x 1¾oz/50g ball
Size 7 (4.5mm) crochet hook

Gauge
Before felting: 13 sts and 18 rows to 4in (10cm) measured over sc using size 7 (4.5mm) hook *or size to obtain correct gauge.*

Abbreviations
See page 13.

Large striped pot
Using size 7 (4.5mm) hook and A, make a drawstring ring (see page 82) and beg as follows:

Round 1 (RS) Draw a loop through center of ring, ch 1, (does NOT count as first st), 8 sc in ring, pull yarn tail to close ring, place marker (see note below). (Do not turn at end of rounds, but work with RS always facing.)
Note: The pots are worked in a spiral, so place a marker at the end of each round to keep track of where each round begins/ends.
Round 2 Ch 1 (does NOT count as first st), 2 sc in first sc, *2 sc in next sc; rep from * 6 times. *16 sc.*
Round 3 Ch 1, 1 sc in first sc, 2 sc in next sc, *1 sc in next sc, 2 sc in next sc; rep from * 6 times. *24 sc.*
Round 4 Ch 1, 1 sc in each of first 2 sc, 2 sc in next sc, *1 sc in each of next 2 sc, 2 sc in next sc; rep from * 6 times. *32 sc.*
Round 5 Ch 1, 1 sc in each of first 3 sc, 2 sc in next sc, *1 sc in each of next 3 sc, 2 sc in next sc; rep from * 6 times. *40 sc.*
Round 6 Ch 1, 1 sc in each of first 4 sc, 2 sc in next sc, *1 sc in each of next 4 sc, 2 sc in next sc; rep from * 6 times. *48 sc.*
Round 7 Ch 1, 1 sc in each of first 5 sc, 2 sc in next sc, *1 sc in each of next 5 sc, 2 sc in next sc; rep from * 6 times. *56 sc.*
Rounds 8 Ch 1, 1 sc in each sc to end.
Rounds 9–12 [Rep round 8] 4 times.
Cutting off and joining in yarns as required, cont in sc and work in stripes as follows:
5 rounds B, 5 rounds A, 5 rounds C, and 5 rounds A. Join with a sl st to first sc of last round. Fasten off.

Medium-size pot with jacquard pattern
Using size 7 (4.5mm) hook and A, work rounds 1–6 as for Large Striped Pot. *48 sc.*
Rounds 7–24 [Rep round 8] 18 times.
Cutting off and joining in yarns as required and working in sc as set, cont as follows:
Round 25 Using C, work in sc to end of round.

Work jacquard pattern (see page 127) as follows:

Rounds 26 and 27 Working in sc, [work 2 sts in A, 2 sts B] 12 times.

Rounds 28 and 29 Working in sc, [work 2 sts in B, 2 sts A] 12 times.

Work 1 round in C and 3 rounds in A. Fasten off.

Small plain pot

Using size 7 (4.5mm) hook and A, work rounds 1–5 as for Large Striped Pot. *40 sc.*

[Rep round 8] 22 times. Fasten off.

Finishing

Darn in any yarn ends.

Put pots and a large towel in washing machine; the towel will help agitate the yarn which aids the felting process. Wash on a normal full cycle at 105°F (40°C). The yarn will not react exactly to same in all washing machines, so check the pot sizes and wash again if necessary to obtain the desired size and density of fabric. Smooth the pots into shape and leave to dry naturally. (See more about felting on pages 176–177).

workshop

five

Making a garment

In the previous Workshops, you have learned how to work different stitches, and how to shape crochet. Following a garment pattern just involves using both these skills at once, but with one key difference—you now have to ensure that your crochet is an accurate size, and what is more, that it will fit your own shape or the shape of the person for whom it is intended.

The two elements that are essential to a good fit are choosing the correct size for your body within the pattern instructions and making a gauge swatch (see page 14) so that your crochet will turn out the same size as that of the person who wrote the pattern. This will ensure the success of your project, and can make all the difference between getting it right the first time and having to correct mistakes or (even worse), undo things later!

Learning new decreasing and increasing techniques

Workshop Five also gives tips for following a crochet pattern successfully and focuses on the decreasing and increasing techniques used to create garment shapes—methods that are much easier to execute than you might imagine.

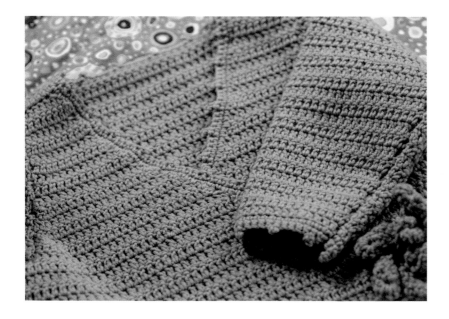

The neck on the Baby Matinee Jacket (see pages 146–149) is shaped by using simple decreasing techniques, and the sleeve by using simple increasing techniques. Making a simple baby garment is a great way for beginners to practice shaping.

Finishing your garment

It is very important when crocheting a garment to make sure that it is finished professionally. This involves blocking and pressing the various pieces when finished (see page 15) and stitching them together carefully (see pages 60–65). Take as much trouble with these and other finishing details (edgings, pockets, collars, buttons, or buttonholes) as you do with your crochet, as they are important ingredients in the overall look of the garment.

In your excitement to create your first garment, you may be tempted to execute finishing touches hastily, but take your time. Well-executed details are essential if you want to enjoy wearing your creation.

Instructions for bobble buttons (top right) and covered buttons (right) are given on pages 154–155. Crocheted buttons can be used on your knitted garments, bags, or pillow covers as well as on your crocheted sweaters and accessories.

Garment instructions

The first thing you need to learn when crocheting a garment is how to choose the correct size for yourself. Every crochet pattern provides the finished measurements of the garment. These are usually standard measurements—circumference around the bust/chest, length from shoulder to hem, and sleeve length. A diagram of the pattern pieces often accompanies the written instructions, which is also marked with measurements (see below).

Most patterns are written in several sizes so that you can choose the one that is most likely to fit you. The difference between the bust/chest measurement and the measurement of finished crocheted garment around the bust/chest is called the "ease." The amount of ease depends on the style of the garment. There will be no "ease," or very little, for a garment designed to be tight-fitting, or a lot of "ease" if it has been designed to be very loose-fitting.

Choosing a size

Take a little time to decide which size to choose for yourself. First, look at the finished measurements of the garment size that corresponds to your bust size. To make sure that this is the size you want to crochet, measure a sweater in your wardrobe that fits you well and is similar in design to the item you want to make—see if this approximates the crocheted finished measurement of your chosen size. Now is your chance to either stick with the size corresponding to your bust measurement, or instead to go for the next size up or down for a more comfortable fit.

Adjustments for fit

Once you have chosen the size you want to follow in the pattern, decide if you want to make any minor adjustments to the garment to achieve a better fit for yourself. Afterall, if you're going to spend time making a garment, you should take the trouble to make sure it suits your body shape as much as possible. When making a top, you can usually very easily lengthen or shorten the body or the sleeves so that they are the perfect fit for you. This does not apply to complicated garment shapes; so if you are a beginner, make sure you only attempt pattern adjustments on garments with simple shapes.

To lengthen or shorten the garment body

If the pattern you have chosen is longer or shorter in the body—or in the sleeve—than you require, you should plan the adjustments before you begin crocheting. To lengthen or shorten a garment, make a note to work more or fewer rows before the armhole shaping is reached. Choose a point in the garment pattern to add or subtract rows; this should be where the garment is worked without shaping for a number of centimeters (inches). If the garment is shaped at the waist, lengthening and shortening is best left to the experts!

To lengthen or shorten the sleeve

The sleeve length can be adjusted in the same way as the body. Make a note to add or subtract rows right after the sleeve shaping has been completed, but before any shaping at the top of the sleeve has begun, so that the changes don't interfere with the fit of the sleeve head into the armhole.

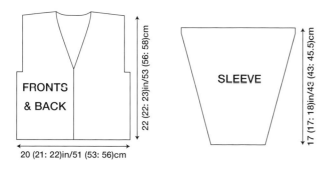

FRONTS & BACK

SLEEVE

22 (22: 23)in/53 (56: 58)cm

17 (17: 18)in/43 (43: 45.5)cm

20 (21: 22)in/51 (53: 56)cm

Measurement diagram pieces

Following your crochet pattern

Once you have chosen the size you want to crochet, you are ready to begin your crochet garment. Before actually making the first foundation chain for the first piece of the garment, read all the information at the beginning of the pattern.

Review the list/s outlining what you need to crochet the garment, and make sure you have enough yarn and the right hook size/s. Extras like buttons, ribbon, or zippers can be purchased later, but if you will be working beads into the fabric, you should have these before you begin. Put the other equipment you will be using in your workbag (see page 11).

If there are any special notes at the beginning of the pattern, read these carefully. Then make your gauge swatch to check that the specified hook will work for you (see below). If necessary, change hook sizes (see page 14 for how to check gauge), as achieving the correct gauge is essential for a successful garment.

Now work all the pieces of the garment in the order they are given in the pattern. When they are complete, follow the finishing instructions with care.

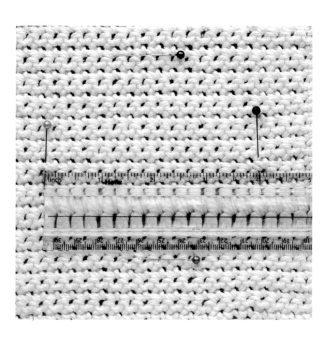

Troubleshooting tips

- Try out pattern instructions, don't just read them and despair that they are too difficult or impossible to follow. Sometimes a pattern doesn't seem to make sense when you are reading through it, but when you are following it step by step with your hook and yarn it works perfectly with no problems at all!

- It's always helpful to have a list of crochet abbreviations handy as you crochet, to remind you what they mean. Many patterns have them all printed at the beginning of the pattern, while for others you have to turn to the beginning or end of the book. If you are working from a photocopy of your pattern (so you can carry it around), remember to copy the abbreviations list as well.

- Make every effort to use the yarn specified in your crochet pattern, as the garment has been very carefully designed to suit this yarn brand. However, if you are determined to use a substitute, choose a yarn as close in texture and thickness to the specified yarn as possible. See page 186 for tips.

- It can be helpful to use a sticky note or ruler to mark where you're up to on the pattern, or make a note on a separate piece of paper. You can also use a stitch counter/clicker to keep track of where you are.

- Experienced crocheters—friends, family, or yarn-store assistants—are always willing to help you with your pattern if you really get stuck!

Decreases for shaping garments

A garment pattern will involve shaping at certain points, and this requires a little more skill than the shaping covered in Workshop Three, where you learned how to work simple decreases in single crochet by simply skipping a stitch and simple increases by working twice into the same stitch (see pages 74–77).

When working stitches that are taller than single crochet, such as half doubles and doubles, you will need to learn further methods of decreasing because simply skipping a stitch would create a visible hole in the fabric. You also need to adapt your shaping techniques to create sharp angles, gentle slopes, or curves.

As decreases generally form the major part of shaping, they are covered first in this section. Your choice of decreasing technique will largely depend on the angle of slope required by the design and the choice of stitch.

Here are some of the common uses for decreasing in garments, including necklines, sleeves, and armholes. There will, of course, be many others, but these demonstrate the ways in which decreasing is used, and the different angles or slopes of decrease that will determine the methods you use.

Neckline decreases

Two typical neckline styles are given on this page, a round neck worked in half double crochet and a V-neck on a cardigan worked in double crochet.

The V-neckline shows how a decrease can be worked on every alternate row to create a front slope for a neckline on a pullover or a cardigan. The decrease used is "double two together" (abbreviated as *dc2tog*), which is explained in detail on page 141.

V-neck decreases

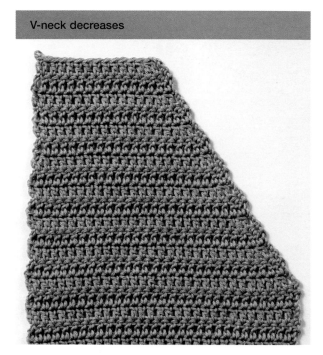

Round-neck decreases

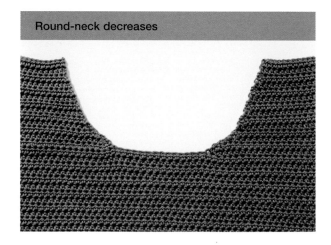

The round neckline illustrates how decreases can be worked on every row, then every other row to create a gentle curve. One side of the neck is worked first and fastened off, then the yarn is rejoined so the other side can be worked in the same way. The decreases used are "half double two together" (*hdc2tog*), which is described on page 140.

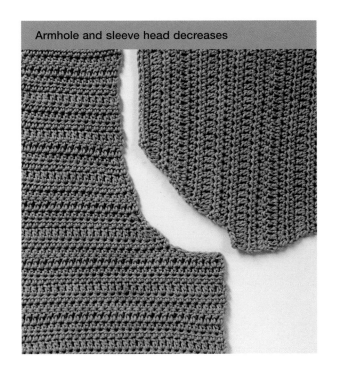

Armhole and sleeve head decreases

Raglan armhole and sleeve decreases

Armhole and sleeve decreases

Here are examples of armhole and sleeve head decreases, and raglan shaping.

The shaped sleeve head and armhole have been designed to fit snugly when they are sewn together (see left). The shaping of both starts with skipped stitches at the edges, and the slopes and curves are then shaped with a variety of double crochet decreases.

Already sewn together with backstitch, the raglan armhole and sleeve shaping are perfectly matched, stripes and all (see below left). The raglan decreases are worked on alternate rows in half double crochet.

Troubleshooting tips

- The most commonly used techniques for decreasing one or two stitches include: sc2tog, sc3tog, hdc2tog, hdc3tog, dc2tog, and dc3tog. Although these decreases are explained on pages 140–141, you do not have to memorize the methods. A crochet pattern will always give full instructions for how to work any decreases (or increases).

- Crochet pattern instructions also provide row-by-row instructions for shaping necklines, sleeves, and armholes. All you need to do is follow these instructions carefully and keep track of where you are in the pattern.

- From time to time (although not always after every increase or decrease row), your pattern will give a stitch count. When a stitch count appears, take the opportunity to count your stitches to make sure you haven't missed or repeated any decreases (or increases).

Working garment decreases

Garment decreases can be worked at the beginning and/or end of a row, a stitch or two in from each edge, or in the middle of a row. The most commonly used method for decreasing one or two stitches in a row is working two or three stitches together as one stitch.

Try out these decreases in single, half double, and double crochet so you will be familiar with them when you first come across them in your crochet pattern. Similar decreases can be worked for most simple stitch patterns and your instructions will guide you through these when they are needed.

Single sc decrease (sc2tog)

Working two single crochet stitches together is a neater way to decrease one stitch than simply skipping a stitch.

To work sc2tog, insert the hook in the next stitch, yo and draw a loop through; then draw a loop through the next stitch in the same way. There are now 3 loops on the hook. Yo and draw through all 3 loops on the hook (see arrow) to complete the single decrease.

Single hdc decrease (hdc2tog)

The principle for working hdc2tog is the same as for sc2tog.

To work hdc2tog, yo and insert the hook in the next stitch, yo and draw a loop through; then do the same in the next stitch. You now have 5 loops on the hook. Yo and draw a loop through all 5 loops on the hook (see arrow) to complete the single decrease.

Double sc decrease (sc3tog)

To decrease two stitches at once in single crochet, insert the hook in the next stitch, yo and draw a loop

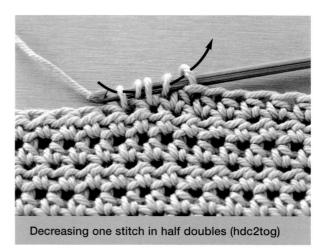
Decreasing one stitch in half doubles (hdc2tog)

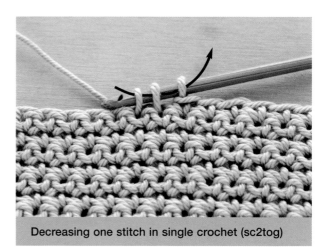
Decreasing one stitch in single crochet (sc2tog)

through; then draw a loop through each of the next 2 stitches in the same way. You now have 4 loops on the hook. Yo and draw through all 4 loops on the hook to complete the double decrease.

Double hdc decrease (hdc3tog)

To decrease two stitches at once in half double crochet, yo and insert the hook in the next stitch, yo and draw a loop through; then do the same in each of the next 2 stitches. You now have 7 loops on the hook. Yo and draw through all 7 loops on the hook to complete the double decrease.

Single dc decrease (dc2tog)

The principle for working two stitches together in double crochet is the same as for single crochet and half double crochet—the next two stitches are worked up to the last yo and then drawn together with one final yo. You will have already come across similar techniques for working clusters or bobbles in textured stitches in Workshop Four.

To work dc2tog, yo and insert the hook in the next stitch, yo and draw a loop through, yo and draw through the first 2 loops on the hook; then do the same in the next stitch. You now have 3 loops on the hook. Yo and draw a loop through all 3 loops on the hook (see arrow) to complete the single decrease.

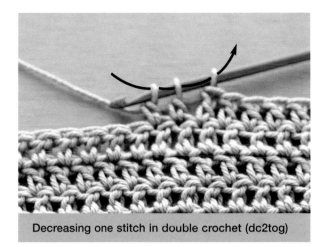

Decreasing one stitch in double crochet (dc2tog)

Double dc decrease (dc2tog)

To decrease two stitches at once in double crochet you work three stitches together, just as for single crochet and half double crochet.

To work dc3tog, yo and insert the hook in the next stitch, yo and draw a loop through, yo and draw through the first 2 loops on the hook; then do the same in each of the next 2 stitches. You now have 4 loops on the hook. Yo and draw a loop through all 4 loops on the hook (see arrow) to complete the double decrease.

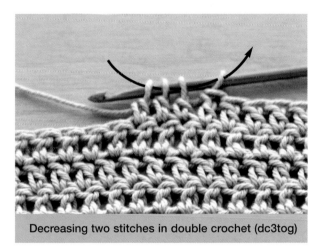

Decreasing two stitches in double crochet (dc3tog)

Decreasing doubles at the beginning and end of a row

When working decreases in double crochet at the beginning of a row, remember that the three turning chains at the beginning of the row will count as your first double crochet stitch. Skip the stitch at the base of your turning chain, then work the decrease over the next two or three stitches as normal.

To decrease at the end of a row of double crochet, you will need to work your decrease, and then work a double crochet into the top of the turning chain, so you need to count backward from the edge of the fabric to work out where to start your decrease stitch. It is especially important to count the number of stitches you have left after a double crochet decrease, to make sure you decreased by correct number of stitches.

Remember that the basic rules of double crochet stitches (and taller stitches) will still apply even when working decreases—always skip the first stitch at the beginning of the row as the turning chain counts as the first stitch of the row, and always work the last stitch into the top of the turning chain at the end of the row. If there is an exception to this rule your pattern will spell it out clearly.

A multi-stitch decrease at at the end of a row

You may need to decrease several stitches at once when shaping a garment, to create a sharp decrease instead of a sloped or curved one. This type of multi-stitch decrease occurs, for example, at the beginning of armhole shaping and sleeve head shaping. Although the technique is the same for all stitches, on tall stitches it creates an abrupt right angle, while on shorter stitches, such as single crochet and half double crochet, it can be integrated into a gentle curve.

1 To decrease several stitches at the end of a row, simply work to the point at which the required number of stitches to decrease are still left unworked on the row as shown, then turn the work.

2 On the following row, work the turning chain, then complete the row in the pattern stitch as normal.

A multi-stitch decrease at the beginning of a row

On some garments, the multi-stitch decrease needs to be worked in the same row on both side edges of the garment piece—to create symmetry. If this is the case, you will need to know how to work a multi-stitch decrease at the beginning of the row as well.

Because a slip stitch is very short, it is useful for moving the hook along the row, without adding any height. This is exactly what you do to decrease a large number stitches at the beginning of a row. Work one turning chain, then for a right-angled decrease, work in slip stitch over the number of stitches you want to decrease and into the position for the first stitch of the row; then work the rest of the row in the usual pattern stitch. For a gentler, curved decrease on half double crochet, you can work a single crochet in the stitch before the first half double of the new row (see right).

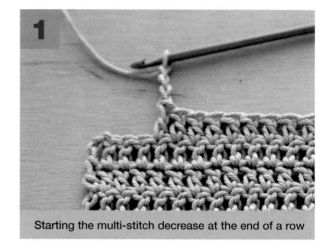
Starting the multi-stitch decrease at the end of a row

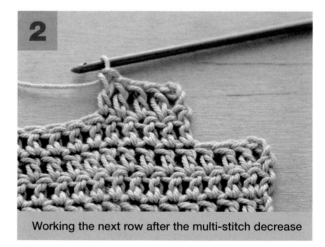
Working the next row after the multi-stitch decrease

Working a curved multi-stitch decrease

Increases for shaping garments

Increases are also used in the shaping of garments and some of them are shown here. In crochet patterns the most common use of increases is for the gradual slope on each side of a sleeve. But you will also come across right-angled increases and shaping formed by using taller and taller stitches across a row.

Sleeve increases

The easiest increasing technique is working more than one stitch into a single stitch (see pages 74–77). This method is used to create the gradual slope on a sleeve, where one stitch is increased at each end of every few rows (see below). For the right-angled increase for a sleeve that is integrated into the body of the garment, a multi-stitch increase is worked (see right and page 144). The technique used for this is the reverse of the multi-stitch decrease.

Fanned skirt-increases

The flared shaping in the sample below is achieved by using stitches of different heights across the vertical rows. This technique can also be used to create flares on other parts of crocheted garments, for example, on collars and cuffs, or for a peplum across the bottom of a woman's jacket. (See page 145 for how to work the fan shaping.)

Right-angled integrated-sleeve increases

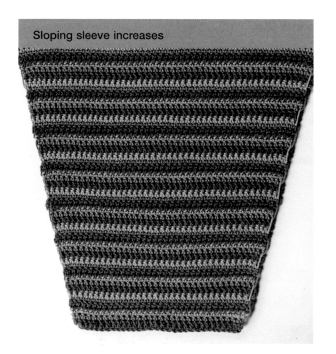
Sloping sleeve increases

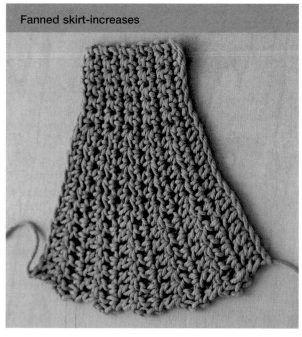
Fanned skirt-increases

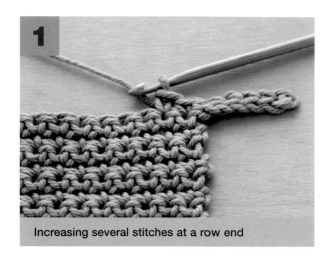

Increasing several stitches at a row end

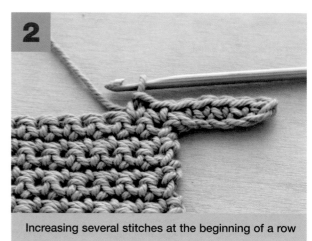

Increasing several stitches at the beginning of a row

Working garment increases

It may be necessary to increase many stitches at the edge of a piece, for example to start sleeves that are worked as one piece with the body of the garment, which are called "integral sleeves" (see page 143).

To create this right-angled increase, you work extra chains—one for each stitch required. For symmetry, the chains needed for each sleeve on the back of the garment (or on the front of a pullover) need to be made on the same row, as explained here.

A multi-stitch increase at each end of a row

1 So that the multi-increases can be worked at both ends of the same row, prepare the chains for the increases at the end of the row on the row *before* the increase row. Begin this row (which will be the end of the increase row) by working the same number of chains as needed for the number of stitches to be increased, plus an extra chain for the turning chain. Work one slip stitch into the second chain from the hook, then one slip stitch into each of the remaining chains and continue across the row as usual as

shown. Because the slip stitches are very short they provide the perfect neutral base for the increased stitches on the next row.

2 At the beginning of the increase row, again work the same number of chains as the number of new stitches you need. For the turning chain, work the number of chains required for the particular stitch you are using for the garment—one chain for the single crochet being worked here. Work across the added chains (see above), then across the row to the slip stitches at the end. For the extra stitches needed at the end of the row, work in the pattern stitch across the slip stitches prepared at the beginning of the last row.

Troubleshooting tip

Another way to add a multi-stitch increase at the end of the row, is to work across a separate length of chain stitches. Use a separate length of yarn to prepare the required number of chains before beginning the increase row, then work across them at the end of the increase row.

Fan shaping

You are now familiar with the differing heights of all the stitches—from slip stitch, which has almost no height, through to the tall treble and beyond. This difference in height can be used to create a scallop edging (see pages 54–55), but some designs also use it to create "fan" (or flared) shaping in the garment—for example, for the flare of the skirt of the Baby Dress (see pages 150–153). Here is a close-up look at how this skirt shaping is achieved.

1 Work the first row of fan shaping by beginning the row with single crochet. When instructed, change to half double crochet stitches and eventually to double crochet stitches. This creates a row that grows gradually and smoothly taller across the row. At the end of the row, work three chains as shown.

2 Work back and forth across each row in the same way, working one single crochet stitch in each single crochet, one half double in each half double, and one double in each double to create a flare in the fabric. (If you do not count the double-stitch turning chains as a stitch and work the doubles only into doubles, the turning chains create an attractive scallop along the edge as here.)

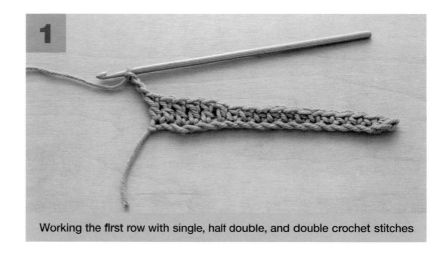

Working the first row with single, half double, and double crochet stitches

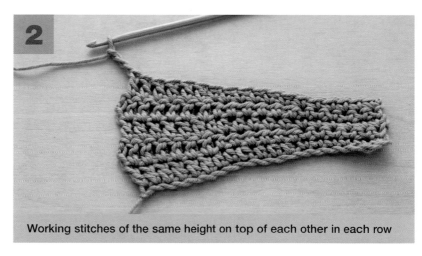

Working stitches of the same height on top of each other in each row

Completed sample of fan shaping

project **eight**

Baby matinee jacket

Worked entirely in doubles, this baby jacket comes in several sizes, so can be made to fit a baby up to the age of 18 months. Making a baby garment is a great way to practice your garment-making skills—the shaping is simple and the project is quickly finished.

Choose the size you want to make by looking at both the age and the chest size it is recommended for. Babies are not all a standard size, so the chest size is given as well as the age for the various sizes. Be careful to follow the instructions for the same size throughout (see page 137 for more on how to follow a crochet garment pattern).

Sizes

To fit age, approximately

0–3	3–6	6–12	12–18	months

To fit chest

16	18	20	22	in
41	46	51	56	cm

Finished measurements

Around chest

17	20	21	24	in
44	51	55	61	cm

Length from shoulder

6	7	9	11	in
16	20	23	28	cm

Sleeve seam

4	6	7	9	in
12	15	19	23	cm

What you need

3 (3: 4: 4) x 1¾oz/50g balls of Rowan *4-Ply Soft* in Tea Rose (401)

Size D-3 (3mm) crochet hook

2 snaps

Blunt-ended yarn needle

Gauge

21 sts and 12 rows to 4in (10cm) measured over dc using size D-3 (3mm) hook *or size necessary to obtain correct gauge*.

Abbreviations

dc2tog = [yo and insert hook in next st, yo and draw a loop through, yo and draw through 2 loops on hook] twice, yo and draw through all 3 loops on hook.

dc3tog = [yo and insert hook in next st, yo and draw a loop through, yo and draw through 2 loops on hook] 3 times, yo and draw through all 4 loops on hook.

See also page 13.

Special shaping notes

All decreases are worked as follows:

To dec 1 st at beg of row: Ch 3 (counts as first dc), skip dc at base of 3-ch, dc2tog over next 2 sts, work in patt to end.

To dec 1 st at end of row: Work in patt to last 3 sts, dc2tog over next 2 sts, 1 dc in top of t-ch at beg of previous row, turn.

To dec 2 sts at beg of row: Ch 3 (counts as first dc), skip dc at base of 3-ch, dc3tog over next 3 sts, work in patt to end.

To dec 2 sts at end of row: Work in patt to last 4 sts, dc3tog over next 3 sts, 1 dc in top of t-ch at beg of previous row, turn.

All increases are worked as follows:

To inc 1 st at beg of row: Ch 3 (counts as first dc), skip dc at base of 3-ch, 2 dc in next dc, work in patt to end.

To inc 1 st at end of row: Work in patt to last 2 sts, 2 dc in next dc, 1 dc in top of t ch at beg of previous row, turn.

Body

The Body is worked in one piece to armholes.

Using size D-3 (3mm) hook, ch 126 (142: 158: 174).

Row 1 (RS) 1 dc in 4th ch from hook, 1 dc in each of rem ch, turn. *124 (140: 156: 172) sts (counting first 3-ch as first dc).*

Row 2 (patt row) Ch 3 (counts as first dc), skip first dc (at base of 3-ch), *1 dc in next dc; rep from * to end, 1 dc in 3rd of 3-ch, turn.

(Last row is repeated to form dc fabric.)

Shape front slopes

Cont in dc, dec 2 sts at each end of next 5 (9: 8: 6) rows, then 0 (0: 1: 1) st at each end of foll 0 (0: 3: 9) rows, ending with WS facing for next row. *104 (104: 118: 130) sts.*

Shape left front

Next row (WS) Ch 3 (counts as first dc), [dc3tog over

next 3 sts] 1 (0: 0: 0) time, [dc2tog over next 2 sts] 0 (1: 1: 1) time, 1 dc in each of next 22 (20: 24: 27) dc and turn, leaving rem sts unworked.

Work on these 24 (22: 26: 29) sts only for left front.

Dec 2 sts at front slope edge of next 4 (0: 0: 0) rows, then 1 st at front slope edge of next 4 (7: 9: 10) rows, then on foll 1 (2: 2: 2) alt rows **and at the same time** dec 1 st at armhole edge of next 3 (4: 5: 6) rows. *8 (9: 10: 11) sts.*

Work 1 row without shaping.

Shape shoulder

Fasten off.

Shape back

Return to last complete row worked, skip next 6 dc, rejoin yarn to next dc and cont as follows:

Next row (WS) Ch 3 (counts as first dc), skip dc at base of 3-ch (this is dc where yarn was rejoined), 1 dc in each of next 39 (45: 51: 57) dc and turn, leaving rem sts unworked.

Work on these 40 (46: 52: 58) sts only for back.

Dec 1 st at each end of next 3 (4: 5: 6) rows. *34 (38: 42: 46) sts.*

Work 6 (6: 7: 7) rows without shaping.

Shape back neck

Next row Ch 3 (counts as first dc), skip first dc, 1 dc in each of next 8 (9: 10: 11) dc and turn, leaving rem sts unworked.

Dec 1 st at neck edge of next row. *8 (9: 10: 11) sts.*

Shape shoulder

Fasten off.

Return to last complete row worked before shaping back neck, skip next 16 (18: 20: 22) dc, rejoin yarn to next dc and cont as follows:

Next row (WS) Ch 3 (counts as first dc), skip dc at base of 3-ch (this is dc where yarn was rejoined), 1 dc in each of next 8 (9: 10: 11) sts, turn.

Dec 1 st at neck edge of next row. *8 (9: 10: 11) sts.*

Shape shoulder

Fasten off.

Shape right front

Return to last complete row worked before dividing for left front and back, skip next 6 dc, rejoin yarn to next dc and cont as foll:

Next row (WS) Ch 3 (counts as first dc), skip dc at base of 3-ch (this is dc where yarn was rejoined), 1 dc in each dc to last 4 (3: 3: 3) sts, [dc3tog over next 3 sts] 1 (0: 0: 0) time, [dc2tog over next 2 sts] 0 (1: 1: 1) time, 1 dc in 3rd of 3-ch, turn. *24 (22: 26: 29) sts.*

Dec 2 sts at front slope edge of next 4 (0: 0: 0) rows, then 1 st at front slope edge of next 4 (7: 9: 10) rows, then on foll 1 (2: 2: 2) alt rows **and at the same time** dec 1 st at armhole edge of next 3 (4: 5: 6) rows. *8 (9: 10: 11) sts.*

Work 1 row without shaping.

Shape shoulder

Fasten off.

Sleeves (make 2)

Using size D-3 (3mm) hook, ch 30 (32: 34: 36).

Work row 1 as given for Body. *28 (30: 32: 34) sts.*

Cont in dc fabric as given for Body, inc 1 st at each end of next 3 (1: 1: 1) rows, then on foll 4 (7: 9: 8) alt rows, then on 0 (0: 0: 2) foll 3rd rows. *42 (46: 52: 56) sts.*

Troubleshooting tips

- If this is the first crochet garment pattern you have ever made, be sure to count your stitches every time there is a stitch count in the pattern—the stitch count is given in italics.

- For a professional finish, work the edgings on the jacket carefully. See pages 52–53 for tips on how to work neat, even single crochet edging stitches.

Work 1 (1: 2: 2) rows without shaping.

Shape top of sleeve

Next row Sl st across and into 4th st, ch 3 (counts as first dc), skip dc at base of 3-ch, 1 dc in each dc to last 3 sts and turn, leaving rem 3 sts unworked. *36 (40: 46: 50) sts.*

Dec 2 sts at each end of next 5 (6: 7: 8) rows. *16 (16: 18: 18) sts.*

Fasten off.

Bow

Using size D-3 (3mm) hook, ch 52.

Next row (WS) 1 sc in 2nd ch from hook, 1 sc in each of next 2 ch, *ch 3, sl st to top of last sc**, 1 sc in each of next 5 ch; rep from * to end, ending last rep at **, 1 sc in each of last 3 ch.

Fasten off.

Finishing

Darn in any yarn ends. Block and press pieces following instructions on yarn label.

Sew shoulder seams.

Front and neck edging

With RS facing and using size D-3 (3mm) hook, join yarn to right front at foundation-ch edge, ch 1 (does NOT count as first st), work 1 row of sc evenly up right front slope, around back neck, and down left front slope to foundation-ch edge (ensuring number of sc worked is a multiple of 5 plus 1), turn.

Next row (WS) Ch 1 (does NOT count as first st), 1 sc in each of first 3 sc, *ch 3, sl st to top of last sc**, 1 sc in each of next 5 sc; rep from * to end, ending last rep at **, 1 sc in each of last 3 sc.

Fasten off.

Cuff edgings (both alike)

Work edging across foundation-ch edge of Sleeve as given for Front and Neck Edging.

Sew sleeve seams. Matching top of sleeve seam to center of skipped sts at underarm and center of last

row of Sleeve to shoulder seam, sew Sleeves into armholes.

Lay one front over other front (left over right for a boy, or right over left for a girl) and sew on snaps to fasten row-end edges of fronts in place.

Tie Bow into a bow and sew to front as shown.

Baby dress

Worked in a soft machine-washable merino wool, this baby dress has been designed to go with the jacket on the previous pages. It is made with single crochet, half double crochet, and double crochet.

   Because the skirt rows are worked vertically, the different stitch heights can be used to create the flare (see page 145). Crocheted onto the finished skirt, the bodice is worked with horizontal rows in the normal way. Personalize this dress by using the color of your choice and a special ribbon.

Sizes

To fit age, approximately

| 0–3 | 3–6 | 6–12 | 12–18 | months |

To fit chest

| 16 | 18 | 20 | 22 | in |
| 41 | 46 | 51 | 56 | cm |

Finished measurements

Around chest

| 18½ | 20½ | 23 | 25 | in |
| 47 | 52 | 58 | 64 | cm |

Length from shoulder to hem

| 11½ | 14 | 16 | 18 | in |
| 29 | 35 | 41 | 46 | cm |

What you need

4 (4: 5: 5) x 1¾oz/50g balls of Rowan *4-Ply Soft* in Tea Rose (401)
Size D-3 (3mm) crochet hook
47in (120cm) of matching satin ribbon

Gauge

21 sts and 12 rows to 4in (10cm) measured over dc using size D-3 (3mm) hook *or size necessary to obtain correct gauge.*

Abbreviations

dc2tog = [yo and insert hook in next st, yo and draw a loop through, yo and draw through 2 loops on hook] twice, yo and draw through all 3 loops on hook.

dc3tog = [yo and insert hook in next st, yo and draw a loop through, yo and draw through 2 loops on hook] 3 times, yo and draw through all 4 loops on hook.

See also page 13.

Dress

The skirt is worked first and then the bodice is worked onto it.

Skirt

Using size D-3 (3mm) hook, ch 32 (42: 53: 61).

Row 1 1 sc in 2nd ch from hook, 1 sc in each of next 8 (11: 14: 17) ch, 1 hdc in each of next 9 (12: 16: 18) ch, 1 dc in each of last 13 (17: 21: 24) ch, turn. *31 (41: 52: 60) sts*.

Row 2 Ch 3 (does NOT count as first st but is used to create a scalloped edge), work 1 dc in each of first 13 (17: 21: 24) dc, 1 hdc in each of next 9 (12: 16: 18) hdc, 1 sc in each of next 9 (12: 15: 18) sc, turn.

Row 3 Ch 1 (does not count as first st), 1 sc in each of first 9 (12: 15: 18) sc, 1 hdc in each of next 9 (12: 16: 18) hdc, 1 dc in each of next 13 (17: 21: 24) dc (do NOT work into top of t-ch of previous row), turn. (Last 2 rows are repeated to form patt.)

Cont in patt until shorter row-end edge (edge with sc, not dc) measures 18½ (20½: 23: 25)in/47 (52: 58: 64)cm, ending after a row 2.

Do not fasten off.

With right sides of edges together, join bottom of first row to top of last row with a slip stitch seam (see page 60).

Fasten off.

Front and back bodice

With double crochet stitches at bottom of skirt and single crochet stitches at top and with RS facing, join yarn to center back seam (seam just made) at top edge and work in rounds as follows:

Round 1 (RS) Join yarn with a sl st to edge at top of center back seam, ch 3 (to count as first dc), then work 97 (109: 121: 133) dc evenly around entire edge (see Note below), join with a sl st to 3rd of 3-ch at beg of round. *98 (110: 122: 134) sts.* (Do not turn at end of rounds, but work with RS always facing.)

Note: To work the doubles evenly around the edge, *[work 1 st in between every row] 5 times, skip 1 row; rep from *—this will give you approximately the right number of stitches, but be sure to count your stitches carefully after round 1 and adjust if necessary.

Round 2 Ch 3 (to count as first dc), 1 dc in each dc to end of round, join with a sl st to 3rd of 3-ch at beg of round. *98 (110: 122: 134) sts.*

Round 3 (eyelet round) Ch 3 (to count as first dc), 1 dc in next dc, *ch 1, skip 1 dc, 1 dc in each of next 2 dc; rep from * to end, join with a sl st to 3rd of 3-ch at beg of round.

Round 4 Ch 3 (to count as first dc), 1 dc in each dc and ch sp to end, join with a sl st to 3rd of 3-ch at beg of round. *98 (110: 122: 134) sts.*

Round 5 Rep round 2.

Fasten off.

Front bodice

With RS facing, skip first 31 (33: 37: 39) sts of next round, join yarn to next dc and beg front bodice as follows:

***Row 1 (RS)** Ch 3 (does NOT count as st), skip dc at base of 3-ch, dc2tog over next 2 dc (2 sts decreased), 1 dc in each of next 31 (39: 43: 51) dc, dc3tog over next 3 dc (2 sts decreased), turn. *33 (41: 45: 53) sts.*

Row 2 Ch 3 (does NOT count as st), skip st at base of 3-ch, dc2tog over next 2 dc, 1 dc in each dc to last 3 sts, dc3tog over last 3 sts, turn. *29 (37: 41: 49) sts.*

Rep last row 0 (1: 1: 2) times more. *29 (33: 37: 41) sts.*

Next row Ch 3 (does NOT count as st), skip st at base of 3-ch (1 st decreased), 1 dc into each dc to last 2 sts, dc2tog over last 2 sts (1 st decreased), turn. Rep last row once more. *25 (29: 33: 37) sts.****

Shape front neck

Next row Ch 3 (counts as first dc), skip st at base of 3-ch, 1 dc in each of first 5 (7: 8: 10) dc, dc2tog over next 2 sts (1 st decreased), turn. *7 (9: 10: 12) sts.*

**Working all decreases as now set, dec 1 st at neck edge of next 2 rows, then on foll 3rd row. *4 (6: 7: 9) sts.* Work 2 (2: 3: 3) rows.

Fasten off.**

Return to last complete row worked before shaping front neck, skip next 9 (9: 11: 11) dc, join yarn to next dc, ch 3 (does NOT count as st), skip dc at base of 3-ch, 1 dc in each st to end, turn. *7 (9: 10: 12) sts.* Work as for first side of neck from ** to **.

Back bodice

Return to last complete round worked before shaping front bodice, skip next 12 (10: 12: 10) dc, rejoin yarn to next dc and work as for front bodice from *** to ***. Work 6 (6: 7: 7) rows.

Shape back neck

Next row Ch 3 (counts as first dc), skip dc at base of 3-ch, 1 dc in each of next 2 (4: 5: 7) dc, dc3tog over next 3 dc, turn. *4 (6: 7: 9) sts.*

Troubleshooting tip

You could wait to buy the ribbon until you have finished the dress. That way you can take the dress with you when choosing your ribbon. If you are making the dress as a gift, why not buy a few different ribbons so they can be changed to match different outfits?

Work 1 row.

Fasten off.

Return to last complete row worked before shaping back neck, skip next 13 (13: 15: 15) dc, join yarn to next dc, ch 3 (does NOT count as st), skip dc at base of 3-ch, dc2tog over next 2 sts, 1 dc in each st to end, turn. *4 (6: 7: 9) sts.*

Work 1 row.

Fasten off.

Finishing

Darn in any yarn ends. Block and press following instructions on yarn label.

Sew shoulder seams.

Armhole edgings (both alike)

With RS facing and using size D-3 (3mm) hook, join yarn to armhole edge at center of sts skipped at underarm, ch 1 (does NOT count as first st), work 1 round of sc evenly around armhole edge, ensuring number of sc worked is a multiple of 5 plus 1, turn.

Next row (WS) Ch 1 (does NOT count as st), 1 sc in each of first 3 sc, *ch 3, sl st to top of last sc**, 1 sc in each of next 5 sc; rep from * to end, ending last rep at **, 1 sc in each of last 3 sc.

Fasten off.

Thread ribbon through eyelet openings on bodice.

Finishing touches

Well-executed finishing touches will give your garment a really professional look, so it is worth taking your time on them. Follow the finishing instructions in your pattern carefully—darning in the yarn ends, blocking the pieces, adding collars, cuffs, or edgings, and stitching the seams in the order described. Here are helpful instructions for making some of the most important finishing touches—buttons, buttonholes, and pockets.

Crocheted buttons

Always choose the buttons for your finished garments with care. The loops or buttonholes on the garment determine the size of the button you need, so take the finished garment with you when buying buttons.

If you prefer, you can crochet your buttons instead of buying ready-made ones. Handmade buttons are a wonderful finishing touch, especially on a gift. Instructions for three different types of crochet buttons are given here for you to experiment with.

Make sure you sew your buttons to the right place on the garment so that they correspond perfectly with the buttonholes or button loops. Badly positioned buttons can ruin the look of the garment.

Bobble button

This is a standard crocheted button. It is filled with toy filling (or leftover yarn) to maintain its round shape. The size of the finished button depends on the thickness of the yarn and the hook size. You can use the same yarn you used for the garment for your button if it is fine enough, or different yarn (or thread) all together. Use a smaller hook than you would use for a garment so that the stitches are worked tightly.

To work the Bobble Button, begin with a drawstring foundation ring (see page 82) and work the Bobble

Button as follows:

Round 1 Insert hook through ring, yo and draw a loop through ring, ch 1, 8 sc in ring, pull yarn end to close ring (do not join to beg of round, but continue in a spiral of rounds).
Round 2 2 sc in each of 8 sc of previous round. *16 sc.*
Round 3 1 sc in each of 16 sc of previous round.
Fill button firmly with toy filling (or yarn).
Round 4 *[Insert hook in next sc, yo and draw a loop through] twice, yo and draw through all 3 loops on hook; rep from * 7 times. *8 sc.*
Fasten off leaving a long yarn tail. Using yarn tail and a blunt-ended yarn needle, weave through sts of last round, pull tight to close, and secure.

Completed bobble button

Beginning round 3 of the ball button

Working round 4 of the ball button

Ball button

This makes an attractive raised button. Try it with a few different yarns to see the effect.

Begin your bobble button with ch 3 and join with a sl st in to first ch to form a ring. Continue as follows:

Round 1 Ch 1, 8 sc in ring, join with a sl st to first sc.

Round 2 Ch 1, [2 sc in next sc] 4 times, join with a sl st to first sc. *16 sc.*

Pull yarn tail at center through center hole to front.

Round 3 Ch 1, [insert hook through center hole, yo and draw through a long loop as shown in *Step 1* above, yo draw though 2 loops] 16 times, join with a sl st to first sc. (The back of the button is facing you.)

Round 4 1 sc in every alternate st as shown in *Step 2* above right, join with a sl st to first sc. *8 sc.*

Fasten off leaving a long yarn tail. Using the yarn tail and a blunt-ended yarn needle, sew a cross at the back to form a base to stitch the button to the garment.

Covered button

You can enclose any ordinary button in a crocheted button cover. Begin the button as for the Bobble Button. Increase stitches in every alternate round until it is big enough to cover the front of the button, insert the button and start rounds of decreasing to cover the back of the button. Finish as for the Bobble Button.

Completed ball button

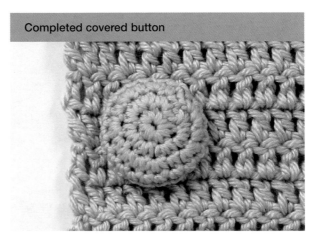

Completed covered button

Buttonholes

The simplest crochet buttonholes are buttonhole loops (see opposite page). They are usually added on to the finished garment piece, and can be used on knitting as well. Aside from the ease of execution, the advantage of buttonhole loops is that you can choose your buttons once the garment pieces are complete and adapt the size of the loops to fit them.

Buttonholes integrated into the crochet, however, are stronger and even easier to make than loops.

Integral buttonholes

Crochet patterns give clear instructions for how and where to incorporate integral buttonholes. For example, if the garment has buttons along a front opening, the front with the buttons on it is worked first and the button positions are marked on it. The front with the buttonholes is worked to match the first front and the buttonholes are inserted to match the button positions.

The simple horizontal buttonhole shown here can also be worked as a separate buttonhole band and stitched to the edge of the front after the garment is complete. Or, the band can be worked vertically onto the edge of the garment front for vertical buttonholes.

Working a simple integral buttonhole
1 On the first row of the buttonhole, work to the position of the buttonhole. Then work two chain stitches (or more, depending on the size of the button), skip the same number of stitches in the row below and continue to the end of the row.

2 On the second row of the buttonhole, work the same number of stitches as those skipped in the previous row into the chain space made for the buttonhole. This creates a smooth and neat buttonhole.

Working the first row of the buttonhole

Working the second row of the buttonhole

Buttonhole loops

Your pattern will always provide exact instructions for how and where to make buttonhole loops. They are usually worked when the edging is added onto the finished pieces. You may need to work a whole series of loops, for example down the front edge of a jacket, or only one loop, for example at the back neck on a baby garment.

Buttonhole loops are so easy to work that you can also add them yourself without the help of a pattern. The button loop can be adapted to fit any size or shape of button by varying the amount of chains worked and the amount of stitches skipped in the edging. If you are improvising, it is a good idea to make a sample to test your button on the loop size before working the loops onto the finished garment piece. The loops stretch slightly after repeated buttoning, so always make them a little tighter than needed for the size of the button.

Make sure you mark the positions of your buttons carefully before beginning the loops. If desired, work an initial row of single crochet along the garment edge as the base for the loop row.

Working a simple buttonhole loop

1 With the right side of the garment facing, work in single crochet until you reach the buttonhole marker. For a large button, work four chains, then skip the last four stitches made and join the chain with a slip stitch to the previous single crochet (see arrow). This forms the loop. (For a smaller button, work fewer chains and join with a slip stitch back into a corresponding stitch.)

2 Then work six single crochet stitches into the loop as shown. (For a buttonhole loop with fewer chains, work fewer single crochet stitches, but ensure that the loop is filled tightly with stitches.) Then continue along on the edge in single crochet until the position for the next button loop is reached.

Joining the loop in place

Working single crochet into the loop

Troubleshooting tip

The technique given here for buttonhole loops is a quick one and makes loops that stand out slightly from the edge of the work. To make loops that sit a little closer to the edging, work the edging in three rows of single crochet. Start with a plain row of single crochet. On the second row work a chain loop for each buttonhole and on the third row fill each loop with single crochet.

Crocheted pockets

Garments can have pockets for practical purposes or as an attractive detail that adds to the overall look of the design, or for both reasons. The two principal types of pocket are the patch pocket, which is stitched onto the garment piece afterward, or the integral pocket, which is crocheted into the main fabric of the garment.

As with buttons and buttonholes, you need to position pockets with care if they are made in pairs so that they line up across the front of the garment.

Other finishing touches

- Remember to block and press your crochet pieces before sewing them in place, just as your pattern instructs you. And always read the yarn label for pressing instructions!

- Crochet collars and cuffs are often added to a garment as a finishing touch. They are usually worked directly onto the neckline or sleeve ends. The instructions for simple edgings on pages 52–53 provide all the help you will need to begin your collar or cuff. Your pattern will give all the row instructions you need for completion of these items or for any shaping involved in making a collar.

- If you want to add a sharply contrasting edging to the row-end edge of a garment piece, it is best to work the first row with the same color as the main garment, then add the contrasting edging. This creates a smoother, neater transition to the new color.

Patch pocket

The patch pocket is the simplest pocket to work, if it is made as a square or rectangle. It is sewn onto the garment using backstitch (see pages 64–65).

A row of single crochet can be worked around the side and bottom edges of the pocket for a smooth all-round edge. More rows of single crochet can then be worked across the top with a smaller hook size to provide a firm pocket top that will not bag out with repeated wear.

A buttonhole worked at the top of the patch pocket (see page 156), with a crocheted button to close it, would make an attractive finishing touch. Alternatively, omit the buttonhole and simply sew a button to the patch pocket as decoration.

Patch pockets offer the opportunity to be creative. You could make a heart-shaped one for a little girl's jacket, or edge the top with embroidered blanket stitch in a contrasting color for a boy's. The simple edgings on pages 56–57 would also make good pocket tops.

A patch pocket decorated with a covered button

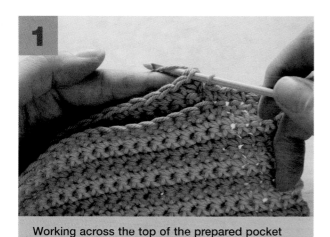
Working across the top of the prepared pocket

Continuing the row across the main garment

Sewing the pocket to the back of the garment

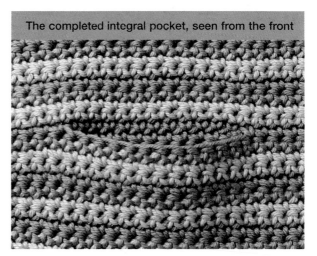
The completed integral pocket, seen from the front

Integral pocket

An integral pocket gives the garment a smart pared-down finish, because the pocket is almost invisible. The pocket lining is worked as a separate piece like the patch pocket, but before the garment is begun. It is then inserted into the main fabric of the garment from behind and crocheted in position, before being stitched down at the back.

As an interesting detail, the pocket lining could be worked in a sharply contrasting color, which would be revealed as the garment was worn and the pockets opened.

Making an integral pocket

1 Work the pocket lining as explained by your pattern and set it aside. Then crochet the main garment to where the top of the pocket is to be positioned. Crochet across the top of the pocket lining as shown, skipping the same number of stitches in the garment.

2 After working across the top of the pocket lining, continue along the main garment fabric.

3 Sew the pocket in place to the wrong side of the garment using overcasting stitches (see pages 64–65).

Woman's cardigan

Worked in a simple textured V-stitch, this short-sleeved cotton cardigan is a perfect cover-up for spring or summer evenings. The zigzag edging is easy to work and adds a great finishing touch. Choose a yarn color that will go with your existing wardrobe.

Sizes

S	M	L	
To fit bust			
32	34	36	in
81	86	91.5	cm
Finished measurements			
Around bust			
38	39	41	in
96	100	104	cm
Length from shoulder			
16½	16½	16½	in
42	42	42	cm
Sleeve seam			
3¼	3¼	3¼	in
8	8	8	cm

What you need

8 (9: 10) x 1¾oz/50g balls of Rowan *4-Ply Cotton* in Cream (153)
Size C-2 (2.5mm) crochet hook
Size D-3 (3mm) crochet hook
5 buttons
Blunt-ended yarn needle

Gauge

30 sts and 17 rows to 4in (10cm) measured over patt using size D-3 (3mm) hook *or size necessary to obtain correct gauge.*

Abbreviations

See page 13.

Back

Using size D-3 (3mm) hook, ch 82 (86: 90) VERY loosely.

Row 1 (RS) Work 1 V-st (of 1 hdc, ch 1, and 1 hdc) in 4th ch from hook (skipped 3-ch counts as 1-ch and 1 hdc), skip next ch, *1 V-st in next ch, skip 1 ch; rep from * to last ch, 1 hdc in last ch, turn. *119 (125: 131) sts—made up of 39 (41: 43) V-sts with 1 hdc at each end of row.*

Row 2 Ch 2 (counts as first hdc), 1 V-st in ch sp at center of first V-st (called *1 V-st in first V-st*), *1 V-st in next V-st; rep from * to end, 1 hdc in 2nd of 3-ch at end of row, turn.

Row 3 (patt row) Ch 2 (counts as first hdc), 1 V-st in each V-st to end, 1 hdc in 2nd of 2-ch at end of row, turn.
(Row 3 is repeated to form patt.)

Shape side-seam edges

Row 4 Ch 2 (counts as first hdc), 1 hdc in first hdc (at base of 2-ch), 1 V-st in each V-st to last st, 2 hdc in 2nd of 2-ch at end of row, turn. *121 (127: 133) sts made up of 39 (41: 43) V-sts with 2 hdc at each end of row.*

Troubleshooting tips

- Be sure to work the foundation chain on the pieces very loosely as instructed. If you find it difficult to work loose chains evenly, use a size larger hook for them.

- You may find that your crochet gauge tightens after you have worked about 4in (10cm) of your piece (this even happens to experienced crocheters), so for a really accurate gauge check, make a gauge swatch 8in (20cm) long.

Rows 5 and 6 Ch 2 (counts as first hdc), skip first hdc, 1 hdc in next hdc, 1 V-st in each V-st to last 2 sts, 1 hdc in last hdc, 1 hdc in 2nd of 2-ch at end of row, turn.

Row 7 Ch 2 (counts as first hdc), 1 hdc in first hdc (at base of 2-ch), 1 hdc in next hdc, 1 V-st in each V-st to last 2 sts, 1 hdc in last hdc, 2 hdc in 2nd of 2-ch at end of row, turn. *123 (129: 135) sts—made up of 39 (41: 43) V-sts with 3 hdc at each end of row.*

Rows 8 and 9 Ch 2 (counts as first hdc), skip first hdc, 1 hdc in each of next 2 hdc, 1 V-st in each V-st to last 3 sts, 1 hdc in each of last 2 hdc, 1 hdc in 2nd of 2-ch at end of row, turn.

Row 10 Ch 2 (counts as first hdc), skip first hdc, 1 V-st in next hdc, 1 V-st in each V-st to last 3 sts, skip next hdc, 1 V-st in next hdc, 1 hdc in 2nd of 2-ch at end of row, turn. *125 (131: 137) sts—made up of 41 (43: 45) V-sts with 1 hdc at each end of row.*

Rows 11 and 12 [Rep row 3] twice.

Rows 13–39 [Rep rows 4–12] 3 times more (noting as you proceed that stitch counts are increasing in each inc row). *143 (149: 155) sts—made up of 47 (49: 51) V-sts with 1 hdc at each end of row.*

Row 40 Rep row 3.

Shape armholes

Row 41 (RS) Ch 1, 1 sl st in each of first 6 sts and in next hdc (2nd hdc of 2nd V-st), 1 V-st in each V-st to last 7 sts, 1 hdc in next hdc, turn. *131 (137: 143) sts—made up of 43 (45: 47) V-sts with 1 hdc at each end of row.*

Row 42 Ch 1, 1 sl st in each of first 3 sts and in next hdc, ch 2 (counts as first hdc), 1 V-st in each V-st to last 4 sts, 1 hdc in next hdc, turn. *125 (131: 137) sts—made up of 41 (43: 45) V-sts with 1 hdc at each end of row.*

Rows 43 and 44 [Rep row 42] twice. *113 (119: 125) sts—made up of 37 (39: 41) V-sts with 1 hdc at each end of row.*

Row 45 Ch 2 (counts as first hdc), 2 hdc in ch sp of first V-st, 1 V-st in each V-st to last 4 sts, 3 hdc in next V-st, turn. *111 (117: 123) sts—made up of 35 (37:*

39) V-sts with 3 hdc at each end of row.

Row 46 Ch 2 (counts as first hdc), skip first 2 hdc, 1 hdc in next hdc, 1 V-st in each V-st to last 3 sts, 1 hdc in each of next 2 hdc, turn. *109 (115: 121) sts—made up of 35 (37: 39) V-sts with 2 hdc at each end of row.*

Row 47 Ch 2 (counts as first hdc), skip first 2 hdc, 1 V-st in each V-st to last 2 sts, 1 hdc in next hdc, turn. *107 (113: 119) sts—made up of 35 (37: 39) V-sts with 1 hdc at each end of row.*

Row 48 Rep row 45.

Row 49 Work in patt across row, turn.

Row 50 Rep row 46.

Row 51 Work in patt across row, turn.

Row 52 Rep row 47.

Row 53 Work in patt across row, turn.

Rows 54–58 Rep rows 48–52. *95 (101: 107) sts—made up of 31 (33: 35) V-sts with 1 hdc at each end of row.*

Work in patt without shaping for 9 rows (rows 59–67), thus ending with WS facing for next row.

Shape back neck

Row 68 (WS) Ch 2 (counts as first hdc), 1 V-st in each of first 10 (11: 12) V-sts, 1 hdc in center of next V-st, turn leaving rem sts unworked. *32 (35: 38) sts—made up of 10 (11: 12) V-sts with 1 hdc at each end of row.* Working on these sts only for first side of neck, cont as follows:

Row 69 Ch 1, 1 sl st in each of first 6 sts and in next hdc, ch 2 (counts as first hdc), 1 V-st in each V-st to last st, 1 hdc in 2nd of 2-ch at end of row, turn. *26 (29: 32) sts—made up of 8 (9: 10) V-sts with 1 hdc at each end of row.*

Row 70 Ch 2 (counts as first hdc), 1 V-st in each of first 6 (7: 8) V-sts, 1 hdc in center of next V-st, turn. *20 (23: 26) sts—made up of 6 (7: 8) V-sts with 1 hdc at each end of row.*

Row 71 Rep row 69. *14 (17: 20) sts—made up of 4 (5: 6) V-sts with 1 hdc at each end of row.* Fasten off.

With WS facing, return to last complete row worked (row 67), skip V-st used for last st of first side of neck and next 9 V-sts, rejoin yarn to center of next V-st by working 1 sl st in ch sp and cont as follows:

Next row (WS) Ch 2 (counts as first hdc), 1 V-st in each V-st to last st, 1 hdc in 2nd of 2-ch at end of row, turn. *32 (35: 38) sts—made up of 10 (11: 12) V-sts with 1 hdc at each end of row.*

Next row Ch 2 (counts as first hdc), 1 V-st in each of first 8 (9: 10) V-sts, 1 hdc in center of next V-st, turn. *26 (29: 32) sts—made up of 8 (9: 10) V-sts with 1 hdc at each end of row.*

Next row Ch 1, 1 sl st in each of first 6 sts and in next hdc, ch 2 (counts as first hdc), 1 V-st in each V-st to last st, 1 hdc in 2nd of 2-ch at end of row, turn. *20 (23: 26) sts—made up of 6 (7: 8) V-sts with 1 hdc at each end of row.*

Rep from ** to **. *14 (17: 20) sts—made up of 4 (5: 6) V-sts with 1 hdc at each end of row.*

Fasten off.

Left front

Using size D-3 (3mm) hook, ch 34 (36: 38) VERY loosely.

Work row 1 as given for Back. *47 (50: 53) sts—made up of 15 (16: 17) V-sts with 1 hdc at each end of row.*

Work rows 2 and 3 as given for Back.

Shape side-seam edge

Cont in patt as set throughout and working all shaping as given for Back, beg shaping as follows:

Inc 1 st at end (side-seam edge) of next row, and then at same edge on every foll 3rd row 11 times more. *59 (62: 65) sts—made up of 19 (20: 21) V-sts with 1 hdc at each end of row.*

Work in patt without shaping for 3 rows.

Shape armhole and front slope

Place marker at beg of last row to denote start of front slope shaping.

Working all shaping as given for Back, cont as follows:

Dec 6 sts at armhole edge (beg) and 1 st at front-slope edge (end) of next row. *52 (55: 58) sts.*

Dec 1 st at front-slope edge and 3 sts at armhole edge of next row. *48 (51: 54) sts.*

Dec 3 sts at armhole edge of next row. *45 (48: 51) sts.*

Dec 1 st at front-slope edge and 3 sts at armhole edge of next row. *41 (44: 47) sts.*

Dec 1 st at each end of next row, then at armhole edge only on foll row. *38 (41: 44) sts.*

Dec 1 st at each end of next row. *36 (39: 42) sts.*

***Dec 1 st at each end of next row and foll alt row. *32 (35: 38) sts.*

Dec 1 st at front-slope edge of next row, armhole edge of foll row, then front-slope edge of next row. *29 (32: 35) sts.*

Rep from *** once more. *22 (25: 28) sts.*

Dec 1 st at front-slope edge only of next row. *21 (24: 27) sts.*

Work in patt without shaping for 1 row.

Dec 1 st at front-slope edge of next 2 rows.

Rep last 3 rows twice more, and then first 2 of these rows again. *14 (17: 20) sts.*

Fasten off.

Right front

Work as given for Left Front, but reversing all shapings.

Sleeves (make 2)

Using size D-3 (3mm) hook, ch 62 VERY loosely.

Work row 1 as given for Back. *89 sts—made up of 29 V-sts with 1 hdc at each end of row.*

Work rows 2 and 3 as given for Back.

Cont in patt as set throughout and working all shaping as given for Back, beg shaping as follows:

Inc 1 st at each end of next row, and then every foll 3rd row twice more, taking inc sts into patt. *95 sts—made up of 31 V-sts with 1 hdc at each end of row.*

Work in patt without shaping for 2 rows.

Shape top of sleeve

Still working all shaping as given for Back, cont as follows:

Dec 6 sts at each end of next row, then 3 sts at each end of foll row. *77 sts—made up of 25 V-sts with 1 hdc at each end of row.*

Dec 1 st at each end of next 23 rows. *31 sts—made up of 9 V-sts with 2 hdc at each end of row.*

Dec 4 sts at each end of next row. *23 sts—made up of 7 V-sts with 1 hdc at each end of row.*

Fasten off.

Finishing

Darn in any yarn ends. Block and press all pieces following instructions on yarn label.

Sew shoulder and side seams using backstitch.

Sew sleeve seams using backstitch, then sew sleeves into armholes.

Cuff edging

With RS facing and using size C-2 (2.5mm) hook, join yarn with a sl st to foundation-ch edge of sleeve at sleeve seam, and work edging as follows:

Round 1 (RS) Ch 1 (does NOT count as first st), work 48 sc evenly around foundation-ch edge of Sleeve (working approximately 2 sc for each V-st), join with a sl st to first sc. (Do not turn at end of rounds, but work with RS always facing.)

Round 2 Ch 4 (counts as 1 dc and 1-ch), skip first 2 sc, *1 dc in next sc, ch 1, skip 1 sc; rep from * to end of round, join with a sl st to 3rd of 4-ch at beg of round.

Round 3 Ch 3 (counts as first dc), 1 dc in first ch sp, *1 dc in next dc, 1 dc in next ch sp; rep from * to end of round, join with a sl st to 3rd of 3-ch at beg of round.

Round 4 Ch 1 (does NOT count as a st), 1 sc in first dc, *skip 2 dc, work [3 dc, ch 3, 3 dc] all in next dc, skip 2 dc**, 1 sc in next dc; rep from * to end, ending last rep at **, join with a sl st to first sc.

Fasten off.

Front edging

Note: To keep edging neat and flat, especially around shoulders and across back neck, it is essential to work the stitches firmly.

With RS facing and using C-2 (2.5mm) hook, join yarn with a sl st to lower edge of Right Front and beg working edging up center edge of Right Front as follows:

Row 1 (RS) Ch 1 (does NOT count as first st), work 57 sc evenly up Right Front to marker (working approximately 3 sc for each pair of row ends), 51 sc up right front slope to shoulder (approximately 3 sc for each pair of row ends), 55 sc across back neck (approximately 5 sc for each pair of V-sts), 51 sc down left front slope to marker (approximately 3 sc for each pair of row ends), and 57 sc evenly down Left Front to lower edge (approximately 3 sc for each pair of row ends), turn. *271 sc.*

Row 2 Ch 3 (counts as first dc), skip first sc, *1 dc in next sc; rep from * to end, turn.

Row 3 Ch 4 (counts as 1 dc and 1-ch), skip first 2 dc, *1 dc in next dc, ch 1, skip 1 dc; rep from * to end, 1 dc in 3rd of 3-ch at end of row, turn.

Row 4 Ch 3 (counts as first dc), 1 dc in first ch sp, *1 dc in next dc, 1 dc in next ch sp; rep from * to end, 1 dc in 3rd of 4-ch at end of row, turn.

Row 5 Ch 1 (does NOT count as a st), 1 sc in first dc, skip 2 dc, work [3 dc, ch 3, 3 dc] all in next dc, skip 2 dc**, 1 sc in next dc; rep from * to end, ending last rep at **, 1 sc in 3rd of 3-ch at end of row.

Fasten off.

Darn in any rem yarn ends.

Sew buttons to edging on Left Front, positioning them opposite chain spaces in edging on Right Front and on every other zigzag point as shown.

workshop

six

Embellishing crochet

This section discusses the various ways you can embellish your crochet: by adding beads both to main fabric or to edgings, by felting the crochet fabric you have created to change its texture, by embroidering on crochet, or by adding fancy crocheted trimmings. Now that you have gained all the basic skills for crochet in the previous workshops, this is the time to really be creative and have fun with your work.

Beads on crochet

With the simple technique of crocheting-in beads you could cover a garment with beads or just add simple bead motifs or patterns along borders. Beaded edgings offer a more subtle use of beads, along a collar, cuff, or the front opening edge of a jacket.

If the holes on the beads you want to use are too small for your crochet yarn, then there's nothing stopping you sewing them on with matching thread—that's how the crochet necklace on pages 174–175 was embellished. Crocheting jewelry is a great way to practice the art of designing. The little motifs will be ready in no time and you can try out very fine crochet hooks for this and use embroidery threads instead of yarns. The crochet flower patterns on pages 86–89 would be suitable for fine crochet jewelry—you would be surprised how different they look when worked in fine threads.

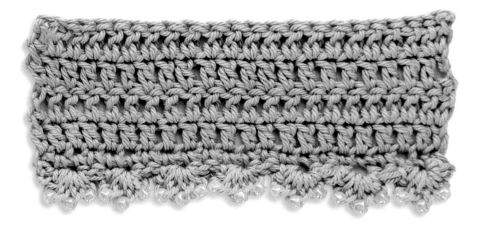

The beads on the Scalloped Bead Edging (left) have been strung on the yarn and worked into the last row of the two-row pattern (see page 172). Each bead is pushed up close to the last stitch between a single crochet and a chain.

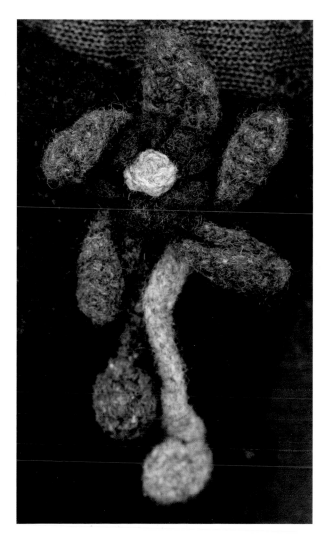

Felting simple crochet motifs (left) completely changes the texture, leaving it hardly recognizable as crochet. If you like to experiment and create original pieces, felting crochet is an area you should explore (see pages 176–177). Alternatively, have fun embellishing various crochet textures by adding appliqué motifs (above) or simple cross, running, or whip stitches (see pages 180–181).

Felting, embroidery, and trimmings

Felting is another area you may want to explore in depth. The softening effect it has on the appearance of crochet is very attractive and would be worth experimenting with. Embroidery need not be as time-consuming as it sounds—the simplest blanket stitch along the edge of your crochet, if worked with a contrasting thick yarn, can transform a design. The same goes for adding a trimming to a plain crocheted pillow, hat, or throw. Embellishments can be elaborate or minimal, depending on your taste, and even the most minimal can have a big impact on your work.

Beading crochet

Adding beads (or sequins) is one of the most popular ways to embellish your crochet. You can crochet-in beads all over the fabric or just along an edging, and the beading technique is very easy to learn.

Choosing beads

Remember when choosing beads for crochet that the bead holes must be big enough for the yarn to pass through easily. Also, if the beads are going to cover the item rather than just a border, make sure that they won't be too heavy for the crochet fabric. When designing your own beaded crochet, always buy only a few beads to start and try them out on a swatch.

Crochet beading technique

1 Thread the beads onto your yarn before you begin the beading so you don't have to cut the yarn to add more beads in the middle of the project. First, thread a sewing needle with a length of thread and knot the ends of the thread together to form a short loop. Pass the end of the yarn through this loop. Then insert the needle into the beads and slide them onto the yarn.

2 Beads can be added to any crochet stitch, but single crochet is being worked here. The beads are added on a wrong side row so that they will sit on the right side of the crochet. Work to the position of the bead, insert the hook through the next stitch, yarn over hook and draw a loop through the stitch. Then push the bead up close to the work, so that the bead fits snugly against the crochet fabric as shown.

3 Complete the single crochet in the usual way. In flat crochet, beads can be added on every alternate row (wrong side rows). When working crochet in the round, however, you can work with the wrong side facing on every row, so you can add beads on every round.

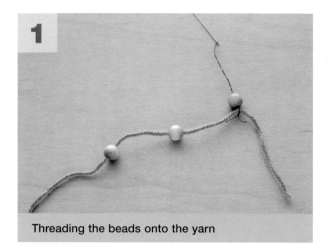

Threading the beads onto the yarn

Pushing the bead into position

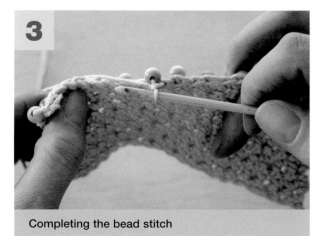

Completing the bead stitch

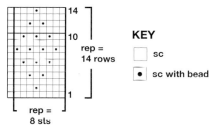

KEY

rep = 14 rows

☐ sc

◉ sc with bead

rep = 8 sts

Working a charted bead pattern

Your crochet pattern will give you instructions for how and where to add the beads. On some patterns the positioning of each bead is explained within the row-by-row instructions as on the beaded edgings on pages 172–173, but on others the bead positions are given on a chart.

The sample above was worked in single crochet, following the chart that accompanies it. Each square on the chart represents a stitch. A bead is pushed up to the crochet fabric in the middle of the single crochet stitch as explained in the technique on the previous page. To work the pattern, read the right-side (odd-numbered) rows from right to left and the wrong-side rows (the even-numbered bead rows) from left to right.

Working beaded edgings

- The technique for adding beads to a crocheted edging is the same as the one given for crochet fabric on the opposite page. Most simple edging patterns will be suitable for beads, and you will find a selection of them on pages 172–173. Don't forget to thread your beads onto the yarn before trying them out.

- Beaded edgings can be worked directly onto knitting, crochet, or fabric as explained for the simple edgings in Workshop Two (see pages 52-57) or worked as separate pieces and sewn on, as for the fancy trimmings on pages 182–185.

- If you're working an edging directly onto a knitted fabric, it looks neater to work into every stitch. If you find that this creates too many stitches (the edging starts to wrinkle and spread out), then you will need to space the stitches out evenly or work two stitches together all along the edge or intermittently (see pages 140 and 141 for how to work sc2tog, hdc2tog, and dc2tog).

- Use an edging with a small repeat if working along a garment edge where you're not sure how many stitches you will end up with. This will make it easier to end a repeat neatly, as you can work a two-stitch repeat into the same stitch at the end, if you run out of stitches.

- Join the yarn on for an edging with a slip stitch or use the slip-knot method explained in Workshop Two on page 52.

Beaded edging patterns

Now that you are familiar with how to work simple edgings (see pages 52–59), you can add beads into the mix! The right edging could make the difference between an ordinary and an extraordinary garment, and the beauty of beaded edgings is that with a little practice, you can transform any edging by simply pushing a bead into place at the chosen point.

Find beads that work with your edging yarn, ensuring that they have holes big enough to thread onto your yarn. Then using the beading techniques on page 170 and the edging tips on page 171, you're ready to start your beaded edging.

Work each of these edgings directly onto crocheted or knitted fabric. Use a matching yarn for the first row of each edging—this is the base row. You can use whatever color you like for the following row/s. Before beginning each edging, thread beads onto the yarn being used for the bead row/s.

Simple bead edging

Row 1 (RS) With RS facing, join yarn with a sl st to beg of edge, ch 1, 1 sc in same place as sl st, then work sc evenly along edge so that there are an odd number of sc in total, turn.
Row 2 Ch 1, 1 sl st in first sc, *ch 1, push bead into position, ch 2, 1 sl st in same place as last sl st, 1 sl st in each of next 2 sc; rep from * to end, ch 1, push bead into position, ch 2, 1 sl st in same place as last sl st. Fasten off.

Chain bead edging

Row 1 (WS) With WS facing, join yarn with a sl st to beg of edge, ch 1, 1 sc in same place as sl st, then work sc evenly along edge so that there are an odd number of sc in total, turn.
Row 2 (RS) Ch 1, 1 sl st in first sc, *ch 2, push 3 beads into position, ch 3, skip 1 sc, 1 sl st in next sc; rep from * to end.
Fasten off.

Triangle bead edging

Row 1 (RS) With RS facing, join yarn with a sl st to beg of edge, ch 3 (to count as first dc), then work dc evenly along edge so that there are a multiple of 5 dc in total, turn.
Row 2 Ch 3, push bead into position—called *bead 1*—, work [1 dc, bead 1, 1 dc, bead 1, 1 dc] all in first dc, skip 3 dc, *1 sc in next dc, ch 3, bead 1, work [1 dc, bead, 1 dc, bead 1, 1 dc] all in next dc, skip 3 dc; rep from * to end, 1 sc in top of t-ch. Fasten off.

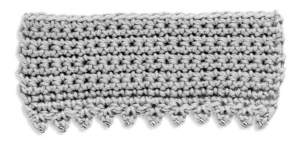

Simple bead edging

Chain bead edging

Triangle bead edging

Looped arch bead edging

Picot arch bead edging

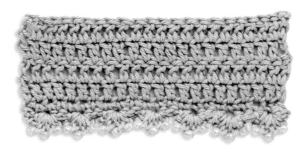

Scalloped bead edging

Looped arch bead edging

Row 1 (WS) With WS facing, join yarn with a sl st to beg of edge, ch 1, 1 sc in same place as sl st, then placing a bead on every alternate sc, work sc evenly along edge so that there are a multiple of 4 sc plus 3 extra in total, turn.

Row 2 Ch 1, 1 sl st in first sc, *ch 5, skip 1 sc, 1 sl st in each of next 3 sc; rep from * to last 2 sc, ch 5, skip 1 sc, 1 sl st in last sc, turn.

Row 3 Ch 1, *work [3 sc, ch 2, push bead into position, ch 1, 1 dc, push bead into position, ch 2, 3 sc] all in next 5-ch space, 1 sl st in center sl st made on previous row between arches; rep from * to end, working 1 sl st in last sl st. Fasten off.

Picot-arch bead edging

Row 1 (RS) With RS facing, join yarn with a sl st to beg of edge, ch 3 (to count as first dc), then work dc evenly along edge so that there are a multiple of 3 dc

plus 1 extra in total, turn.

Row 2 Ch 5, skip first 3 dc, 1 dc in next dc, *ch 3, skip next 2 dc, 1 dc in next dc; rep from * to end, working last dc of last rep in top of t-ch, turn.

Row 3 Ch 1, 1 sc in first ch sp, *ch 4, push bead into position, ch 2, 1 sl st in 4th ch from hook, ch 2, 1 sc in next ch sp; rep from * to end.

Fasten off.

Scalloped bead edging

Row 1 (RS) With RS facing, join yarn with a sl st to beg of edge, ch 1, 1 sc in same place as sl st, then work sc evenly along edge so that there are a multiple of 3 sc in total, turn.

Row 2 Ch 1, 1 sl st in first sc, *work [(1 sc, push bead into position, ch 1) 3 times, 1 sc] all in next sc, 1 sl st in each of next 2 sc; rep from * to last 2 sc, work [(1 sc, push bead into position, ch 1) 3 times, 1 sc] all in next sc, 1 sl st in last sc. Fasten off.

project **eleven**

Crochet necklace

The circle motifs of this simple necklace are sewn on once the motifs are completed, so you can arrange them as you like and you can use tiny beads that cannot be threaded onto thick yarn. Making crochet jewelry is ideal for using up yarn scraps. Simply choose colors to match a favorite outfit.

Size

The finished necklace measures approximately 17in (43cm) long, but can be made to any desired length.

What you need

Small amount of Rowan *Cotton Glace* in each of 3 colors as follows:

A   Dawn Grey (831) or Twilight (829)
B   Ecru (725)
C   Shoot (814)

Size D-3 (3mm) crochet hook
2 abalone buttons, 9mm in diameter
49 clear 3mm glass beads
33 gray 2mm glass beads
12 green 3.5mm glass beads
Matching sewing thread to sew on beads
Jewelry materials—20in (51cm) of tiger tail (or other fine stiff necklace wire of desired length), necklace clasp, 6 jump rings, and 2 crimp beads (to secure wire ends in place)

Gauge

The large circle motif measures 2⅛in (5.5cm) in diameter and the small circle motifs 1⅛in (3cm) in diameter using size D-3 (3mm) hook.

Abbreviations

See page 13.

Large circle motif

Using size D-3 (3mm) hook and A, ch 7 and join with a sl st to first ch to form a ring.

Round 1 Ch 1 (does NOT count as first st), 15 sc in ring, join with a sl st to first sc.

Round 2 Ch 1, 1 sc in each sc to end, join with a sl st to first sc. Fasten off A.

Round 3 Join B with a sl st to any sc, ch 1, 2 sc in same place as sl st, *2 sc in next sc; rep from * to end, join with a sl st to first sc. *30 sc.* Fasten off B.

Round 4 Join C with a sl st to any sc, ch 1, 1 sc in same place as sl st, *1 sc in next sc; rep from * to end, join with a sl st to first sc.

Round 5 Ch 1, 2 sc in first sc, ch 2, skip next 2 sc, *2 sc in next sc, ch 2, skip next 2 sc; rep from * to end of round, join with a sl st to first sc. Fasten off C.

Round 6 Join A with a sl st to any ch sp, ch 1, 3 sc in same ch sp as sl st, ch 2, *3 sc in next ch space, ch 2; rep from * to end of round, join with a sl st to first sc. Fasten off.

Small circle motifs (make 2)

Using size D-3 (3mm) hook and B, ch 5 and join with a sl st to first ch to form a ring.

Round 1 Ch 1, 12 sc in ring, join with a sl st to to first sc. Fasten off B.

Round 2 Join A with a sl st to any sc, ch 1 (does NOT count as first st), 1 sc in same place as sl st, ch 1, skip next sc, *1 sc in next sc, ch 1, skip next sc; rep from * to end, join with a sl st to first sc. Fasten off A.

Round 3 Join C to any ch sp, ch 1, 2 sc in same place as sl st, ch 2, *2 sc in next ch sp, ch 2; rep from * to end, join with a sl st to first sc. Fasten off.

Finishing

Darn in yarn ends on motifs.
With right side of large motif facing, sew 7 clear

beads evenly spaced on top of stitches of round 1; sew 15 gray beads evenly spaced on top of stitches of round 3; and sew 10 clear beads to stitches of round 6 (one on top of each of group of 3-sc). With right side of each small motif facing, sew on 6 gray beads evenly spaced between rounds 1 and 2.

Necklace assembly

Attach one jump ring to top of one stitch on edge of each small motif. Attach one jump ring to one hole of each button, and one jump ring to end of clasp.

Cut a piece of tiger tail (or other stiff necklace wire) 2in (5cm) longer than desired finished length. Push wire through center of two stitches on wrong side of round 6 of large motif and slide motif to middle of wire. Then to *each side* of large motif, thread on *3 clear beads, 1 gray bead, 3 clear beads, 1 green bead*, 1 button, 1 green bead, rep from * to *, then thread on 1 green bead, 1 small motif, 1 green bead, 3 clear beads, 1 gray bead, and 1 clear bead.

Attach one end of necklace wire to jump ring on clasp and other end to remaining jump ring so that the necklace is the desired length. Use crimp beads to secure ends of wire, placing 2 green beads over each wire loop attached to jump ring.

Felting crochet

Felt is one of the oldest fabric types in the world. It is made by simply washing a 100 percent wool fabric in hot soapy water and agitating the fibers together—either by rubbing by hand or by washing in the washing machine. This mats, tangles, and shrinks the wool fibers to create a soft, dense fabric. Any stripes or patterns are softened and blended, and the piece shrinks. Whether knitted, crocheted, or woven, felted fabric can be cut without fraying, as the fibers are so dense.

Single crochet forms a dense fabric anyway, and when felted it becomes even denser. This is perfect for bags, hats, and containers. Washing in a normal full 105°F (40°C) cycle in a washing machine is the quickest way to felt crocheted fabric. It's best to put the crochet in the felting wash with some other items, for example a few towels, as this will increase the agitation and help the felting process. Bear in mind, however, that how much you put in with the crochet will affect how much it shrinks—the fewer other items in the wash, the less the wool will felt. Start with

caution when felting in the washing machine—you can always shrink it more, but you can't make it bigger once it has shrunk! After felting, smooth out the crochet and leave it to dry naturally.

The samples here show how felting affects some simple crochet textures. All are worked in Rowan *Scottish Tweed DK* using a size 7 (4.5mm) crochet hook. Remember to choose a non-machine-washable wool yarn for your crochet felting experiments.

Felted stripes

You can see how simple stripes look before and after felting. The felting shrinks the swatch more in width than length and gently blurs the stripe pattern.

Felted puffballs

Because of its highly raised surface, Puffball Stitch is a perfect candidate for felting as you can see from the unfelted and felted samples. Work it as follows:
Make a multiple of 6 ch.
Row 1 (WS) 1 sc in 2nd ch from hook, 1 sc in each of rem ch, turn.

Unfelted stripes

Felted stripes

Unfelted Puffball Stitch

Felted Puffball Stitch

Rows 2 Ch 1 (does NOT count as first st), 1 sc in each st to end, turn.

Row 3 Rep row 2.

Row 4 Ch 1, 1 sc in each of first 5 sc, *ch 1, work [1 dc in next st 2 rows below] 6 times all in same st, take hook out of last dc, insert it in first ch of this group, pull lp of last dc through the ch—called 1 puffball—, skip this last sc, 1 sc in each of next

5 sc; rep from * to end, turn.

Rows 5–7 [Rep row 2] 3 times.

Row 8 Ch 1, 1 sc in each of first 2 sc, *ch 1, 1 puffball below next sc (skip this sc), 1 sc in each of next 5 sc; rep from * to last 3 sts, 1 puffball below next sc, 1 sc in each of last 2 sc.

Row 9 Rep row 2.

Rep rows 2–9 to form patt.

Felted jacquard

In bicolor jacquard the yarn not in use is carried across the row inside the other stitches (see page 127). This is why it will shrink a little more widthwise than stitches that use only one color in a row. The effect of felting on jacquard really softens the appearance of the pattern, so this is a technique that is worth exploring with your felting skills. And remember, you can cut the felted crochet into shapes without it fraying.

Unfelted jacquard

Felted jacquard

177

project **twelve**

Felted bag with corsage

Felted single crochet is perfect for making bags as it creates a very firm fabric. The felting also softens the appearance of the surface texture.

The Clematis crocheted flower on pages 87–88 was used here for the corsage, but you could use any of the flowers in Workshop Three to decorate your bag. Just make sure you use a wool yarn so that it will felt properly.

Size

The finished bag when felted measures approximately 8in (20cm) by 8in (20cm), although the size may vary slightly due to the felting process and according to the washing machine used.

What you need

Rowan *Scottish Tweed DK* in three colors as follows:

A	Thistle (016)	2 x 1¾oz/50g balls
B	Indigo (031)	1 x 1¾oz/50g ball
C	Autumn (029)	1 x 1¾oz/50g ball

Size 7 (4.5mm) crochet hook
Blunt-ended yarn needle

Gauge

Before felting: 13 sts and 18 rows to 4in (10cm) measured over sc using size 7 (4.5mm) hook *or size necessary to obtain correct gauge*.

Abbreviations

See page 13.

Main bag

Using size 7 (4.5mm) hook and A, ch 34.
Row 1 1 sc in 2nd chain from hook, 1 sc in each of rem ch, turn. *33 sc.*

Row 2 Ch 1 (does NOT count as first st), 1 sc in each sc to end, turn.
(Last row when repeated forms sc patt.)
Work 91 rows more in sc. Fasten off.
At one short side of piece fold corners in toward center to create a point (this will be top flap) and pin. Sew center seam on point and sew horizontal edge of point to bag.

Ties (make 2)

Using size 7 (4.5mm) hook, join A with a sl st to point of flap and ch 21, then work 1 sc in 2nd ch from hook, 1 sc in each of rem ch, join with a sl st to flap.
Fasten off.
Make another tie in same way, but do not join to bag.

Flower

Work flower as for the Clematis flower on pages 87–88, using size 7 (4.5mm) hook and B for petals, A for center flower, and C for center spot.

Short dangling bobble

Make a drawstring ring (see page 82) and using size 7 (4.5mm) hook and B, beg rounds as follows:
Round 1 Insert hook through ring and draw a loop through ring, ch 1, 5 sc in ring, pull yarn tail to close ring, join with as sl st to first sc of round.
Round 2 Ch 1, 2 sc in each sc to end of round, join with as sl st to first sc of round. *10 sc.*
Round 3 Ch 1, 1 sc in each sc to end of round, join with as sl st to first sc of round.
Round 4 Ch 1, skip first sc, 1 sc in next sc, *skip next sc, 1 sc in next sc; rep * to end of round, stuff bobble with scrap of yarn, then join with a sl st to opposite side and pull tight to close top of bobble.
Do not fasten off.

Bobble stem

Ch 11, then work 1 sc in 2nd ch from
hook, 1 sc in each of rem ch, join with
a sl st to bobble. Fasten off.

Long dangling bobbles
(make 2)

Using A for first and C for 2nd, make
as for Short Dangling Bobble, but begin
bobble stem with ch 21.

Handle

Using size 7 (4.5mm) hook and A,
ch 187.
Row 1 1 sc in 2nd ch from hook, 1 sc
in each of rem ch, then continuing
along other side of foundation ch, 1 sc
in each of next 186 ch. Fasten off.

Felting

Darn in any yarns ends. Then wash all
pieces in the washing machine on a full
105°F (40°C) cycle. (See page 176 for
tips on felting.) Smooth out and leave
to dry naturally.

Finishing

With right sides together, fold up of
straight edge of Bag piece by about 8in
(20cm) and pin in place. Sew side
seams, then sew each end of handle to
a side seam. Turn Bag right side out
and press into shape.
Sew ends of Dangling Bobbles to flap
as shown, then sew Flower on top of
these ends. Sew separate Tie to front
of Bag to correspond with position of
Tie on flap.

Embroidering crochet

Crocheted fabric provides a good firm base for embroidery and appliqué. Whip stitch, cross-stitch, and running stitch are all good choices for the embroidery as can all be worked on crochet using the grid of the crochet stitches as a guide to positioning. The samples on the opposite page are given to inspire you to create your own designs. Try the simple stitches as explained here, and then why not make a base swatch of single crochet and have some fun experimenting with other embroidery stitches and textured yarns to see what effects you can produce?

The appliqué technique could also be used on a T-shirt or knitted garment, and you can appliqué any design you'd like. For example, a long crochet cord could be twisted to create a stem, and this could be surrounded with crocheted flowers and leaves to create a forest of plants! Or, small flowers could be added around the neck or hem of a garment for a delicate edging. (See pages 84–89 for crochet flower and leaf patterns.)

When working embroidery on crochet or sewing motifs to crochet, remember to use a blunt-ended yarn needle. You probably wouldn't want to cover a whole garment or even pillow cover with embroidery, but it can be used sparingly to great effect to create borders or small areas of interest.

Cross-stitch

Single crochet is a good ground for cross-stitches because the individual stitches are fairly square just like the cross-stitches. A close toning color was used for the cross-stitch embroidery shown, for a subtle effect, but worked in strongly contrasting colors it would give a vibrant feel.

Begin by making a square swatch of single crochet. Then using a single strand of the same yarn you used for the single crochet, but in a contrasting color, work a cross-stitch over every other single crochet across a row. Leave three rows unworked, then work another row of cross-stitches, and continue in this way to achieve the effect shown.

Crochet flower appliqué

You can apply crocheted motifs to any kind of crochet base. The swatch shown here was worked in Up and Down Stitch (see page 110) and the Eight-Petal Flower on page 123 was used for the large motif. Work the smaller flower in the same way, but make the ring with five chains and work three chains for the petals in round 2, instead of five. For the little circles, work eight single crochet into a drawstring ring (see page 82). Make as many motifs as you like and scatter them across the fabric. Pin them in position, then sew them in place using only a few stab stitches at the centers. The three-dimensional effect is enhanced if the edges of the motifs are left free.

Running stitch

This is a simple hand stitch that can used in many ways, depending on your skills or on the look you wish to achieve.

The swatch shown has been worked in a stripe in close-toned colors using single crochet for one two-row stripe and half double crochet for the other two-row stripe. A simpler effect could be achieved by working the crochet ground in one color and then using a boldly contrasting color for the running stitch.

Use two strands of yarn for the running stitch embroidery so that it stands out from the ground. Work the running stitches over one single crochet stitch at a time between the rows for neat, even embroidery. Repeat the horizontal running stitches between every other pair of rows so that some of the crochet texture is left exposed.

Cross-stitches on single crochet

Appliqué on a textured stitch

Running stitch on single crochet stripes

Whip stitch on raised half doubles

Whip stitch

Whip stitch is perfect for working on stitches with vertical lines, for example vertical jacquard stripes or raised doubles.

To make the swatch shown above, work the base fabric in Rib Stitch (see page 110). Use the same yarn you used for the crocheted swatch for the embroidery, but use a contrasting color and two strands held together so that the embroidery will stand out. Cover some of the vertical rows of single crochet stitches between the raised doubles with the short diagonal stitches of whip stitch.

Fancy trimming patterns

You were introduced to simple edgings in Workshop Two (see pages 52–59) and beaded edgings on pages 170–173, but here's the chance to go one step further, with decorative trimmings and edgings with tassels and bobbles attached. These can be used in many ways, for example, for the edge of a skirt, cardigan, or sweater to make the simplest style look unique. What about laying a trimming on a skirt hem and stitching it in place, or using as a trimming around the crown of a hat, or as decoration on a simple jacket? You could even glue an edging onto a lampshade for the total crochet experience in the home!

Some trimmings that could be used as an "insertion" have also been included, for example the Zigzag Trimming. This could be inserted in between two pieces of woven or knitted fabric, then you could thread ribbon through the holes, for extra decoration or to use as a drawstring.

Instructions are also given here for adding tassels straight onto crocheted (or knitted) fabric for a scarf, decoration on a child's sweater, or simply added to a cozy afghan to throw over the sofa. Just use your imagination and see how far it can take you! (For a reminder of how to crochet onto a knitted, woven, or crocheted fabric, refer back to Workshop Two (see pages 52–59).

Zigzag trimming

Make a foundation ch of the required length that has a multiple of 4 ch plus 2.
Row 1 1 sc in 2nd ch from hook, 1 sc in each of rem ch to end, turn.
Row 2 (RS) Ch 4, skip first 2 sc, *leaving last loop of each st on hook, work 2 tr in next sc, yo and draw

through all 3 loops on hook—called *tr cluster*—, ch 3, tr cluster in same sc as before, *skip next 3 sc, work [tr cluster, ch 3, tr cluster] all in next sc; rep from * to last 2 sc, 1 tr in last sc, turn.
Row 3 Ch 1, 1 sc in first tr, *1 sc in top of next cluster, 2 sc in next 3-ch space, 1 sc in top of next cluster; rep from * to end, 1 sc in 4th of 4-ch.
Fasten off.

Tassels on crochet fabric

Cut a piece of cardboard that is about 1½in (4cm) wider than the desired finished tassel length. For the first tassel, wind the yarn around the cardboard at least 10 times—adjust the number of times you wind the yarn depending on the yarn thickness and how plump you want the tassel to be. Cut through the yarn at one end so that you have 10 strands of yarn of equal length. Keeping the strands aligned, fold them in half. Then insert a crochet hook from back to front through the edge of the crochet fabric, pull the folded ends through to the back, creating a loop. Pull the cut ends through this loop and pull tight to create a tassel. Make all the remaining tassels in the same way, spacing them out evenly along the edge.

Seashell trimming

Ch 6 and join with a sl st to first ch to form a ring.
Row 1 Ch 3, 5 dc in ring, ch 4, 1 sc in ring, turn.
Row 2 Ch 3, 5 dc in 4-ch space, ch 4, 1 sc in 4-ch space, turn.
Rep row 2 until trimming is required length.
Fasten off.

Crossover bobble trimming

This is a madcap trimming, great for the home—

pillows or throws—or what about making a simple cardigan and adding this trimming to it? It's simpler than it looks, but worth the effort. The crochet balls are made last and crocheted onto the completed braid (see page 184).

Braid

Work a foundation ch of the required length that has a multiple of 4 ch plus 1.

Row 1 1 sc in 2nd ch from hook, 1 sc in each of rem ch, turn.

Row 2 Ch 1 (does NOT count as first st), 1 sc in each sc to end, turn.

Row 3 Ch 4, skip first sc, *leaving last loop of each st on hook, work 9 dc in next st, yo and draw through all 10 loops on hook to complete bobble, ch 1 very tightly to hold bobble, ch 1, skip next sc, 1 dc in next sc**, ch 1, skip next sc; rep from *, ending last rep at **, turn.

Row 4 Ch 1, 1 sc in first dc, *1 sc in next ch space, 1 sc in top of next bobble, 1 sc in next ch space, 1 sc in next dc; rep from * to end, working last sc of last rep in 3rd of 4-ch, turn.

Row 5 Rep row 2. Fasten off.

Crochet balls

Before making each ball, make the stuffing for each ball as follows.

Stuffing

Take a short length of matching yarn and roll it around the end of

Zigzag trimming

Tassels on crochet fabric

Seashell trimming

Troubleshooting tip

The Seashell Trimming is a good candidate for beads (see pages 170–171 for bead techniques). For a subtle effect, you could add one bead on every row between the last of the first "3-ch" and the first double.

Crossover bobble trimming

Eyelet-hole trimming with tassels

Troubleshooting tip

The technique used for the tassel eyelets on the Eyelet-Hole Trimming can be adapted for use on other straight-edged trimmings. Just make the chain loops in the last row big enough for your tassels.

your finger to create a small ball, then wrap the cut end around this and push it into the center to hold it in place.

First ball

Make a drawstring ring (see page 82) and begin rounds as follows:

Round 1 Insert hook through ring and draw a loop through ring, ch 1, 8 sc in ring, pull yarn tail to close ring, place marker (a marker is placed at the end of each round to indicate where each round ends/begins).

Round 2 2 sc in each of next 8 sc, place marker. *16 sc.*

Round 3 1 sc in each of next 16 sc, place marker. Insert stuffing in ball.

Round 4 [Insert hook in next sc, yo and draw a loop through] twice, yo and draw through all 3 loops on hook; rep from * 7 times, place marker. *8 sc.*

Round 5 1 sc in each of next 8 sc. [Take loop off hook, insert hook in next st and draw a loop through it] 8 times to close top. *1 loop now on hook.*

Do NOT cut off yarn.

Attach first ball to braid

Working either from right to left or left to right on braid, ch 9, join with a sl st to foundation-ch edge of braid below first bobble on braid, 1 sl st in each of 9-ch just made (working back to ball), work another ch 9, skip next bobble on braid, join with a sl st to edge of braid below next bobble on braid, 1 sl st in each of 9 ch just made (working back to ball). Fasten off and sew yarn tail into ball to finish.

Remaining balls

Make and attach next ball in same way, but join it first to edge of braid below skipped bobble on braid, then skip next bobble and join other end to edge of braid below next bobble along (see photo).

Continue making and attaching balls in this way until the balls are all joined on in a cross-over design.

Eyelet-hole edging with tassels

This edging would make an attractive border for a crocheted, knitted, or fabric blanket.

Edging

Make a foundation ch of the required length that has a multiple of 4 ch.

Row 1 (RS) 1 sc in 2nd ch from hook, 1 sc in each of rem ch, turn.

Row 2 Ch 1 (does NOT count as first st), 1 sc in each sc to end, turn.

Row 3 Ch 3 (counts as first dc), skip first sc, 1 dc in next sc, *ch 2, skip next 2 sc, 1 dc in each of next 2 sc; rep from * to last sc, 1 dc in last sc, turn.

Row 2 Ch 1 (does NOT count as first st), 1 sc each of first 3 dc, *2 sc in next 2-ch space, 1 sc in each of next 2 dc; rep from *end, working last sc of last rep in 3rd of 3-ch, turn.

Row 5 Ch 6, skip first 2 sc, 1 sl st in next sc, *ch 3, skip next sc, 1 sl st in next sc, ch 6, skip next sc, 1 sl st in next sc; rep from * to end.

Fasten off.

Tassels

Make individual tassels as explained for Tassels on Crochet Fabric (see page 182) and attach one to each 6-ch loop created on last row of edging.

Sewing trimmings in place

- Take the time to sew your trimmings in place carefully. Start by pinning them to the woven fabric, knitting, or crochet that you are embellishing. Ease it into place if it is slightly too long, or stretch it out gently if it is a little too short (but not so much that it pulls in the base fabric).

- Next, using a contrasting sewing thread and a sewing needle, baste the trimming and remove the pins. The best results are always achieved with basting because the thread can be caught on the pins and the basting stitches hold the trimming much more firmly than pins. It seems like it takes longer to baste something in place, but in the end it saves time!

- If you are sewing the trimming to knitting or crochet, use matching yarn and a blunt-ended yarn needle to sew it in place. Catch the trimming in position with neat overcast stitches (see pages 64–65) or short invisible running stitches.

- Use a matching sewing thread and a sewing needle with a sharp point if you are joining the trimming to a woven fabric. You can use any hand stitch you like for this, but try to make the stitches small and invisible on the right side of the piece.

- Once the trimming has been neatly secured in place, remove the basting stitches and lightly press the trimming on the wrong side including the stitches you have just worked.

Yarn information

For the best results, use the specified Rowan yarns for the projects in this book. If, however, you wish to find a substitute, use a yarn that matches the original in type, and buy according to length of yarn per ball, rather than by the weight of the ball.

Yarn descriptions

Descriptions of the yarns used in this book are given below. The gauge for stockinette stitch is provided for each yarn because this gives an accurate guide to the thickness of the yarn when you are trying to find a substitute (more accurate than crochet gauges).

The Standard Yarn Weight System developed by the Craft Yarn Council of America is also a helpful guide for finding yarn substitutes of similar weights (see opposite page). The system classifies yarn weights into different categories and gives approximate gauge ranges for each category. It also provides guidance as to which crochet hook sizes go with which yarn-weight category, which is handy if you want to try out a yarn for crochet.

Where shade numbers are given in this book, they are only suggestions. There can be no guarantee that every color will still be available by the time you use this book, as shades change frequently with trends.

Rowan Cotton Glace

A fine-weight cotton yarn; 100 percent cotton; 126yd (115m) per 1¾oz/50g ball; recommended gauge—23 sts and 32 rows to 4in (10cm) measured over St st using size 3–5 (3.25–3.75mm) knitting needles.

Rowan Denim

A lightweight cotton yarn; 100 percent cotton; 102yd (93m) per 1¾oz/50g ball; recommended gauge—20 sts and 28 rows (before washing) and 20 sts and 32 rows (after washing) to 4in (10cm) measured over St st using size 6 (4mm) knitting needles.

Rowan 4-Ply Cotton

A super-fine-weight cotton yarn; 100 percent cotton; approximately 186yd (170m) per 1¾oz/50g ball; recommended gauge—27–29 sts and 37–39 rows to 4in (10cm) measured over St st using size 3 (3mm) knitting needles.

Rowan 4-Ply Soft

A super-fine-weight wool yarn; 100 percent merino wool; 191yd (175m) per 1¾oz/50g ball; recommended gauge—28 sts and 36 rows to 4in (10cm) measured over St st using size 3 (3.25mm) knitting needles.

Rowan Handknit Cotton

A lightweight cotton yarn; 100 percent cotton; 93yd (85m) per 1¾oz/50g ball; recommended gauge—19–20 sts and 28 rows to 4in (10cm) measured over St st using size 6–7 (4–4.5mm) knitting needles.

Rowan Kidsilk Haze

A fine-weight mohair yarn; 70 percent super kid mohair and 30 percent silk; 229yd (210m) per ⅞oz/25g ball; recommended gauge—18–25 sts and 23–34 rows to 4in (10cm) over St st using size 3–8 (3.25–5mm) knitting needles.

(continued on page 188)

Standard yarn-weight system

Categories of yarn, gauge ranges, and recommended hook and needle sizes from the Craft Yarn Council of America.
YarnStandards.com

Yarn-weight symbol and category names	**0** LACE	**1** SUPER FINE	**2** FINE	**3** LIGHT	**4** MEDIUM	**5** BULKY	**6** SUPER BULKY
Types of yarns** in category	10-count crochet thread, fingering	sock, fingering, baby	sport, baby	DK, light worsted	worsted, afghan, Aran	chunky, craft, rug	bulky, roving
Crochet gauge ranges* in single crochet to 4in (10cm)	32–42*** (double crochet sts)	21–32 sts	16–20 sts	12–17 sts	11–14 sts	8–11 sts	5–9 sts
Recommended hook in metric size range	1–2.25 mm	2.25–3.5 mm	3.5–4.5 mm	4.5–5.5 mm	5.5–6.5 mm	6.5–9 mm	9mm and larger
Recommended hook in US size range	8, 7, 6 steels to B-1	B-1 to E-4	E-4 to 7	7 to I-9	I-9 to K-10½	K-10½ to M-13	M-13 and larger
Knit gauge ranges* in St st to 4in (10cm)	33–40*** sts	27–32 sts	23–26 sts	21–24 sts	16–20 sts	12–15 sts	6–11 sts
Recommended needle in metric size range	1.5–2.25 mm	2.25–3.25 mm	3.25–3.75 mm	3.7.5–4.5 mm	4.5–5.5 mm	5.5–8 mm	8mm and larger
Recommended needle in US size range	000 to 1	1 to 3	3 to 5	5 to 7	7 to 9	9 to 11	11 and larger

* GUIDELINES ONLY: The above reflect the most commonly used gauges and hook or needle sizes for specific yarn categories.

** The generic yarn-weight names in the yarn categories include those commonly used in the US and UK.

*** Ultra-fine lace-weight yarns are difficult to put into gauge ranges; always follow the gauge given in your pattern.

Rowan Pure Wool DK

A lightweight yarn; 100 percent super-wash wool yarn; approximately 137yd (125m) per 1¾oz/50g ball; recommended gauge—22 sts and 30 rows to 4in (10cm) measured over St st using size 6 (4mm) knitting needles.

Rowan RYC Cashsoft DK

A lightweight wool-and-cashmere-mix yarn; 57 percent extra fine merino wool, 33 percent microfiber, 10 percent cashmere; approximately 142yd (130m) per 1¾oz/50g ball; recommended gauge—22 sts and 30 rows to 4in (10cm) measured over St st using size 6 (4mm) knitting needles.

Rowan Scottish Tweed DK

A lightweight wool yarn; 100 percent pure new wool; approximately 123yd (113m) per 1¾oz/50g ball; recommended gauge—20–22 sts and 28–30 rows to 4in (10cm) measured over St st using size 6 (4mm) knitting needles.

Rowan Yarn addresses

Contact the distributors listed here to find a supplier of Rowan handknitting yarns near you, or contact the main office in the UK or the Rowan websites: **www.knitrowan.com** or **www.rowanclassic.com**

USA: Westminster Fibers Inc., 165 Ledge Street, Nashua, NH 03060.
Tel: 1-800-445-9276.
E-mail: rowan@westminsterfibers.com
www.westminsterfibers.com

AUSTRALIA: Australian Country Spinners, 314 Albert Street, Brunswick, Victoria 3056.
Tel: (61) 3 9380 3888. Fax: (61) 3 9387 2674.
E-mail: sales@auspinners.com.au

AUSTRIA: Coats Harlander GmbH, Autokaderstrasse 31, A-1230 Wien.
Tel: (01) 27716-0. Fax: (01) 27716-228.

BELGIUM: Coats Benelux, Ring Oost 14A, Ninove, 9400. Tel: 0346 35 37 00.
E-mail: sales.coatsninove@coats.com

CANADA: Same as USA.

CHINA: Coats Shanghai Ltd., No. 9 Building, Boasheng Road, Songjiang Industrial Zone, Shanghai, 201613. Tel: (86-21) 5774 3733. Fax: (86-21) 5774 3768.

DENMARK: Coats HP A/S, Nannagade 28, 2200 Kobenhavn N. Tel: 35 86 90 50. Fax: 35 82 15 10.
E-mail: info@hpgruppen.dk www.hpgruppen.dk

FINLAND: Coats Opti Oy, Ketjutie 3, 04220 Kerava.
Tel: (358) 9 274 871. Fax: (358) 9 2748 7330.
E-mail: coatsopti.sales@coats.com

FRANCE: Coats France/Steiner Fréres, SAS 100 avenue du Général de Gaulle, 18 500 Mehun-Sur-Yèvre.
Tel: 02 48 23 12 30. Fax: 02 48 23 12 40.

GERMANY: Coats GMbH, Kaiserstrasse 1, D-79341 Kenzingen. Tel: 7644 8020. Fax: 7644 802399. www.coatsgmbh.de

HOLLAND: Same as Belgium.

HONG KONG: Coats China Holding Ltd., 19/F

Millenium City 2, 378 Kwun Tong Road, Kwun Tong, Kowloon. Tel: (852) 2798 6886. Fax: (852) 2305 0311.

ICELAND: Storkurinn, Laugavegi 59, 101 Reykjavek. Tel: (354) 551 8258. E-mail: storkurinn@simnet.is

ITALY: Coats Cucirini srl, Via Sarca 223, 20126 Milano. Tel: 800 992377. Fax: 0266111701. E-mail: servizio.clienti@coats.com

JAPAN: Puppy-Jardin Co. Ltd., 3-8 11 Kudanminami, Chiyodaku, Hiei Kudan Bldg. 5F, Tokyo. Tel: (81) 3 3222-7076. Fax: (81) 3 3222-7066. E-mail: info@rowan-jaeger.com

KOREA: Coats Korea Co. Ltd., 5F Kuckdong B/D, 935-40 Bangbae-Dong, Seocho-Gu, Seoul. Tel: (82) 2 521 6262. Fax: (82) 2 521 5181.

LEBANON: y.knot, Saifi Village, Mkhalissiya Street 162, Beirut. Tel: (961) 1 992211. Fax: (961) 1 315553. E-mail: yknot@cyberia.net.lb

LUXEMBERG: Same as Belgium.

MEXICO: Estambres Crochet SA de CV, Aaron Saenz 1891-7, Monterrey, NL 64650. Tel: +52 (81) 8335-3870.

NEW ZEALAND: ACS New Zealand, 1 March Place, Belfast, Christchurch. Tel: 64-3-323-6665. Fax: 64-3-323-6660.

NORWAY: Coats Knappehuset AS, Pb 100 Ulset, 5873 Bergen. Tel: (47) 55 53 93 00. Fax: (47) 55 53 93 93.

PORTUGAL: Apartado 444, 4431958 Vila Nova de Gaia. Tel: (351) 2237 70773. Fax: (351) 2237 70705. E-mail: elvira.castro@coats.com

SINGAPORE: Golden Dragon Store, 101 Upper Cross Street #02-51, People's Park Centre, Singapore 058357. Tel: (65) 6 5358454. Fax: (65) 6 2216278. E-mail: gdscraft@hotmail.com

SOUTH AFRICA: Arthur Bales PTY, P.O. BOX 44644, 62 4th Avenue, Linden 2104. Tel: (27) 11 888 2401. Fax: (27) 11 782 6137.

SPAIN: Oyambre, Pau Claris 145, 80009 Barcelona. Tel: (34) 670 011957. Fax: (34) 93 4872672. E-mail: oyambre@oyambreonline.com Coats Fabra, Santa Adria 20, 08030 Barcelona. Tel: 93 2908400. Fax: 93 2908409. E-mail: atencion.clientes@coats.com

SWEDEN: Coats Expotex AB, Division Craft, Box 297, 401 24 Göteborg. Tel: (46) 33 720 79 00. Fax: (46) 31 47 16 50.

SWITZERLAND: Coats Stroppel AG, Stroppelstrasse 16, CH-5300 Tungi (AG). Tel: 056 298 12 20. Fax: 056 298 12 50.

TAIWAN: Cactus Quality Co. Ltd., P.O. Box 30 485, Taipei. Office: 7Fl-2, No 140, Roosevelt Road, Sec 2, Taipei. Tel: 886-2-23656527. Fax: 886-2-23656503. E-mail: cqcl@m17.hinet.net

THAILAND: Global Wide Trading, 10 Lad Prao Soi 88, Bangkok 10310. Tel: 00 662 933 9019. Fax: 00 662 933 9110. E-mail: theneedleworld@yahoo.com

UK: Rowan, Green Lane Mill, Holmfirth, West Yorkshire HD9 2DX, England. Tel: +44 (0) 1484 681881. Fax: +44 (0) 1484 687920. E-mail: mail@knitrowan.com

Index

Acknowledgements

The publishers would like to thank the following for their help with this book: Sally Harding for editorial work, Anne Wilson for the design, John Heseltine for the photography, Penny Hill and Sue Whiting for pattern checking, Emma Seddon and Càrole Downie for crocheting, Juliette Manning and Tara Heseltine for modeling, Ed Berry for photoshop work.

They would also like to thank the following for the project designs:

Emma Seddon (page 42, Four-Stitch Coaster; page 50, Striped Mixed-Yarn Scarf; page 66, Patchwork Pillow Cover; page 90, Cloche Hat with Flower; page 102, Wagon Wheel Throw; page 122, Crochet Belt; page 130, Felted Pots; page 150, Baby Dress; page 178, Felted Bag with Corsage)

Lois Daykin (page 146; Baby Matinee Jacket)

Kim Hargreaves (page 160, Woman's Cardigan)

Sarah Hazell (page 174, Crochet Necklace)